Divide

By Michael Robbins   Photographed by Paul Chesley
Prepared by the Special Publications Division
National Geographic Society   Washington, D.C.

High Country Trail:
Along The Continental Divide

By Michael Robbins

Photographed by Paul Chesley

Published by
  The National Geographic Society
  Gilbert M. Grosvenor, *President*
  Melvin M. Payne, *Chairman of the Board*
  Owen R. Anderson, *Executive Vice President*
  Robert L. Breeden, *Vice President, Publications
    and Educational Media*
Prepared by
  The Special Publications Division
  Donald J. Crump, *Editor*
  Philip B. Silcott, *Associate Editor*
  William L. Allen, William R. Gray, *Senior
    Editors*
Staff for this Book
  Ron Fisher, *Managing Editor*
  John Agnone, *Picture Editor*
  Suez B. Kehl, *Art Director*
  Louisa Magzanian, *Senior Researcher;* Amy
    Goodwin, *Researcher;* Suzanne Nave Patrick,
    Research Assistance
Illustrations and Design
  Cynthia B. Scudder, *Assistant Designer*
  Richard Fletcher, *Design Assistant*
  John D. Garst, Jr., Margaret Deane Gray,
    Gary M. Johnson, Tibor G. Toth, *Map
    Research, Design, and Production*
  Leslie B. Allen, Jane H. Buxton, Jacqueline
    Geschickter, Paul D. Martin, Jane R.
    McCauley, Joseph Reap, Suzanne Venino,
    Picture Legend Writers
Engraving, Printing, and Product Manufacture
  Robert W. Messer, *Manager*
  George V. White, *Production Manager*
  Mark R. Dunlevy, *Production Project Manager*
  Richard A. McClure, Raja D. Murshed,
    Christine A. Roberts, David V. Showers,
    Gregory Storer, *Assistant Production
    Managers*
  Susan M. Oehler, *Production Staff Assistant*
  Debra A. Antonini, Nancy F. Berry, Pamela A.
    Black, Barbara Bricks, Nettie Burke, Jane
    H. Buxton, Mary Elizabeth Davis, Claire M.
    Doig, Rosamund Garner, Victoria D.
    Garrett, Karen E. Gibbs, Nancy J. Harvey,
    Joan Hurst, Suzanne J. Jacobson, Artemis S.
    Lampathakis, Virginia A. McCoy, Merrick P.
    Murdock, Cleo Petroff, Victoria I. Piscopo,
    Carol A. Rocheleau, Katheryn M. Slocum,
    Jenny Takacs, Phyllis C. Watt, *Staff
    Assistants*
Colleen B. DiPaul, Martha K. Hightower, *Index*

Library of Congress CIP Data: page 197

*Grandeur on an awesome scale confronts fire lookout
Brian Stricker. Brian lived with this front-yard vision
of Mount Wilbur while on summer duty at his post on
the Continental Divide in Glacier National Park.
PRECEDING PAGES: La Ventana — the Window —
opens in the knife-edged Divide in the San Juan
Mountains of Colorado. PAGE 1: In Glacier, Clements
Mountain rises beyond an alpine meadow lush with
moss and wildflowers. HARDCOVER: Hikers often
encounter mountain goats in the northern Rockies.*

Horse-packers plod upward through a light mist on the Continental Divide in
Colorado. The author and photographer logged hundreds of miles along the Divide—

Contents

*on foot, horseback, skis, snowshoes, "even
on a dogsled and on a white-water raft."*

Prologue

ONE AFTERNOON I raced a rolling storm across boulder flats above Spring Creek Pass in the San Juan Mountains and reached shelter just as lightning began flickering behind me.

On another day, in the long blue shadows of a sub-zero sunrise, I skied a wind-scoured summit in Colorado, plunging down rock-walled chutes of glistening powder snow—the deepest I'd ever seen.

In Montana, nooning on a brittle rock rim above Swiftcurrent Glacier with my back to the dry wind, I looked down on glacial lakes of ultramarine. Each successive, distant pool was paler than the one before it. Suspended rock flour, which had been pulverized by the glaciers, tinted the waters less and less the farther they were from the Continental Divide, the source of the powdered rock.

On different days I knelt and drank from the trickling sources of three rivers: the Rio Grande, the Colorado, and the Missouri.

The Continental Divide is a matter of water. It is also an idea, at once a geographer's abstract concept and a solid reality. It is a dashed line on maps of the West, and a place high in the mountains where you can stand and watch waters part at your feet.

The Continental Divide extends from South America through Alaska. In the contiguous United States, it is a cold, wild, lonely, and hazardous strip of largely mountainous country that reaches from Mexico to Canada. Precipitation that falls here runs down one slope or the other, east or west, into the Atlantic drainage or the Pacific drainage. The Continental Divide is a barrier to travel, a shaper of weather, a vantage, and one long extreme.

The entire Divide itself cannot be hiked. Even when all 3,100 miles of the Continental Divide Trail are completely plotted, cleared, and signed into existence, the trail will coincide with the Divide only about 20 percent of the time. One need view just a few miles of, say, the Bitterroot Range on the Idaho-Montana line, where the Divide is a broken, battlemented rim of peaks and jagged ridges, to see that only an adroit and energetic mountain goat could hope to move directly along the Divide.

Once, in Glacier National Park, photographer Paul Chesley and I left the trail and climbed up to a rough section of the Divide itself to sight along its peaks. There on a barren flat we could look along a mile of rugged ridge. Again and again the Continental Divide described a pattern of horizontal and vertical lines that was as rigidly geometric as a dense city skyline. The best mountaineer in the world might devote weeks to following a dozen miles of the Divide in such terrain.

Long before it was a challenge to ambitious hikers, the Continental Divide was a formidable hurdle to westering travelers. Sensible

Swollen with spring snowmelt from high in the San Juan Mountains, Cascade Falls spills a veil of water near Ouray, Colorado.

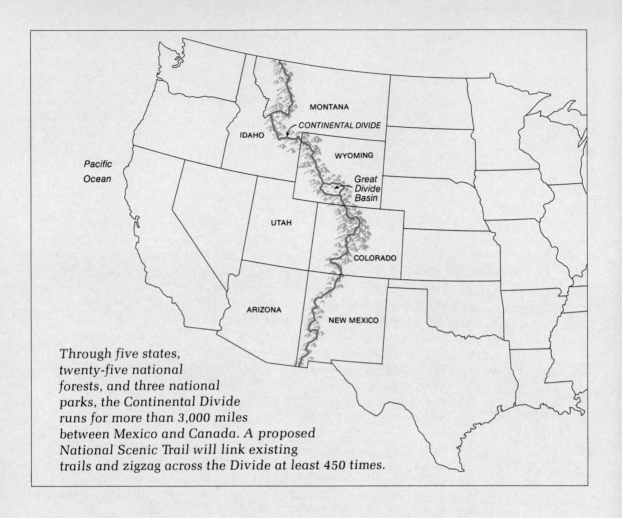

Through five states,
twenty-five national
forests, and three national
parks, the Continental Divide
runs for more than 3,000 miles
between Mexico and Canada. A proposed
National Scenic Trail will link existing
trails and zigzag across the Divide at least 450 times.

trappers and settlers soon learned to skirt isolated mountain ranges, but the Divide was a height no one could avoid. After Lewis and Clark, generations of restless Americans headed upstream on the great rivers, still dreaming of a Northwest Passage. Wyoming's South Pass, crossed by the mountain men in the early 1800s, was the closest thing to realization of that dream. Broad and nearly flat, it was the best way through the Rockies. The Divide was crossed first on foot and horseback, then on wagon wheels, and eventually with rails and pavement. But it never has been easy.

Trails *along* the Continental Divide, rather than over it, are a newer notion. Traditional pack trails have been in use for years. A segment of Continental Divide trail was developed by the Civilian Conservation Corps in the 1930s. Much of the high country is marked by mining roads, sheep driveways, U.S. Forest Service roads, and logging traces. In the three national parks along the way, there are many hiking trails in sight of the Divide.

The idea of a single, unified, border-to-border, nonstop Continental Divide Trail was formally proposed first in a 1966 Bureau of Outdoor Recreation report, *Trails for America*. It recommended a system of national scenic trails, including one along the Divide. In 1968 Congress passed the National Trails System Act, which recognized the first two major trails—the Appalachian and the Pacific Crest —and proposed the study of others. Congress added to this system in 1978 with an amendment that gave the trail official status. As proposed in a Department of the Interior study, it will be a pathway up the Rockies, passing through five states and incorporating the existing, discontinuous trails and primitive roadways. Except in New Mexico, nearly all of it will be on public land.

Today the existing trails along the Divide are being drawn together into a unit under forest service coordination. As of 1981, some 1,480 miles of trails had been selected for probable inclusion in the system, but the entire process may take years. Until then, the continuous, border-to-border Continental Divide Trail remains an idea and a partially realized dream.

The Continental Divide etches a line through resources of incalculable richness. In country where each mile brings the sights and sounds of teeming life—from snow buttercups to ponderosa pines, from pocket mice to grizzly bears—there are miles and miles of desert, pine forest, alpine fastness, and high plains. Hundreds of these miles are in national parks and national forests. It is impossible to quantify, perhaps even to comprehend, such delights.

Already some people have hiked all the miles from Mexico to Canada, and as the trail develops more will surely do so. That is a special feat, a sustained performance of will involving months of time and much planning, resources, and muscle. I've met some who did it as a quest, a venture into unknown days and places, a spiritual journey. But that is not how most people will touch or be touched by the Continental Divide Trail. Most will venture along for a few miles or for a few days and nights from a handy trail head, and they will have a compact but rewarding experience.

Paul Chesley and I had never met before accepting this assignment. During our months together, through quiet miles and shared good times, we formed a deep friendship. That is one of the best things that can happen on a long trail. We measured many hundreds of miles on foot, on horseback, on skis, on snowshoes, even on a dogsled and on a white-water raft.

My previous outdoor experience was in exploring and camping around the Great Lakes and in the Appalachians, with some ventures into the Sierra Nevada and parts of the Rockies. Paul grew up on a Minnesota farm and has lived in the Colorado Rockies for years. His experience with horses and with high elevations gave us a head start. The subtleties of wilderness experience he shared with me ensured not only our survival and safety, but also a measure of comfort.

Now when I think about the Continental Divide, I think about the clouds observed, the rain tasted, the ice felt. We got very cold, very hot, very wet, sometimes all in a single day. Long ago a friend who favors horse-packing in the mountains told me about "shining times," when you're warm under the sun and cool in the breeze, when you're breathing bright air and riding so high you can see down all around you. The Continental Divide is a place for shining times.

PRECEDING PAGES: *Swooping arch of sandstone creates Echo Amphitheater, a place of unearthly beauty and eerie sound effects in northern New Mexico.*

Trinity Peaks *emerge like a jagged row of teeth from the shadow of the Continental Divide in Colorado. Long a challenge*

14

to climbers, these forbidding
mountains reach well above 13,000
feet. A dusting of new snow
accents their geological scars.

FOLLOWING PAGES: High on a slope
of Wyoming's Wind River Range, a tightly
grouped herd of Rocky Mountain elk moves
to lower ground within its winter range.

PRECEDING PAGES: Like an artist's palette, Grand Prismatic Spring colors the landscape of Yellowstone National Park in Wyoming. A boardwalk brings visitors to its edge.

Peaceful meadow dotted with groundsel offers a hiker a change from high country trails a few miles from the Divide in

Yellowstone. Many animals, including grizzlies, visit such lushly vegetated spots after the park's rigorous winters.

FOLLOWING PAGES: *Along a ridge sheared by a slow-moving mass of ice, the Divide stairsteps to the crest of Gunsight Mountain in Montana's Glacier National Park.*

1 New Mexico:

In New Mexico early morning shadows darken the ruins of Pueblo

The First Steps

IN MAY the sun rises early over the Alamo Hueco Mountains, and soon after six o'clock the strong light hits a lonely border station at Antelope Wells, New Mexico. A dirt road crosses a combination cattle guard and international gate. The nearest towns of any size lie several dusty hours' drive south in Mexico or north in New Mexico. Customs officers here often see only a single car a day.

Antelope Wells is as close as you can drive to the intersection of the Mexican border and the Continental Divide. Here you can make some final telephone calls and top off your water bottles. Even in the spring the days are hot, so it is best to start early. If you hike the Continental Divide from Mexico to Canada, this is where you take your first step.

Because photographer Paul Chesley and I wanted to take our first step at the green sign at the border that reads "0 Miles," we began our journey just east of the Divide and across the line in Mexico. We were greeted there by affable *jefe de inmigración* Carlos Johnson. When we told him where we were headed, he laughed: "Long way!" But he and an American official, Ruby Madera-Font, pushed open the gate for us, wished us well, and we set off.

When we began our northward trek, no Continental Divide Trail as such existed in much of New Mexico. The Divide itself measures 800 miles across the state, and there are stretches of hiking trail on or near it. Unlike other high country states, New Mexico has no national parks and only three national forests along the Continental Divide, and there are few good hiking trails on the ranches, the public lands, or the Indian reservations that account for most of the mileage.

The Divide crosses the U.S.-Mexico border west of Antelope Wells, follows the Animas Mountains, loops across miles of flat desert, then climbs into the Burro Mountains and the Pinos Altos Range near Silver City. In the Gila National Forest and the Black Range, good trails follow the Divide. It swings to the northeast, then back west in a long bight around the vast Plains of San Agustin.

It crosses the Tularosa and Mangas mountain ranges, then continues north across semiarid grasslands and zones of piñons and junipers. Edging the Zuni Mountains and the Malpais lava flow, it runs westward through the Cibola National Forest, then swings straight northeastward across more desert and cuts a corner of the Jicarilla Apache Indian Reservation. Near Cuba the Divide turns north into the Badland Hills and traverses forest highlands into Colorado.

Though there is scarcely a mile that is not in—or in sight of—mountains, the Divide touches more sharply contrasting terrain in New Mexico than in any other state.

From Antelope Wells, Paul and I followed ranch roads that paralleled the border westward across several miles of hot flats to the actual Continental Divide in the San Luis (Continued on page 34)

Snaking through western New Mexico, the Continental Divide traverses an 800-mile mosaic of varying landscapes. From the Mexican border, hikers cross sun-bleached desert, climb mountains to high plateaus, and wind through shadowy forests.

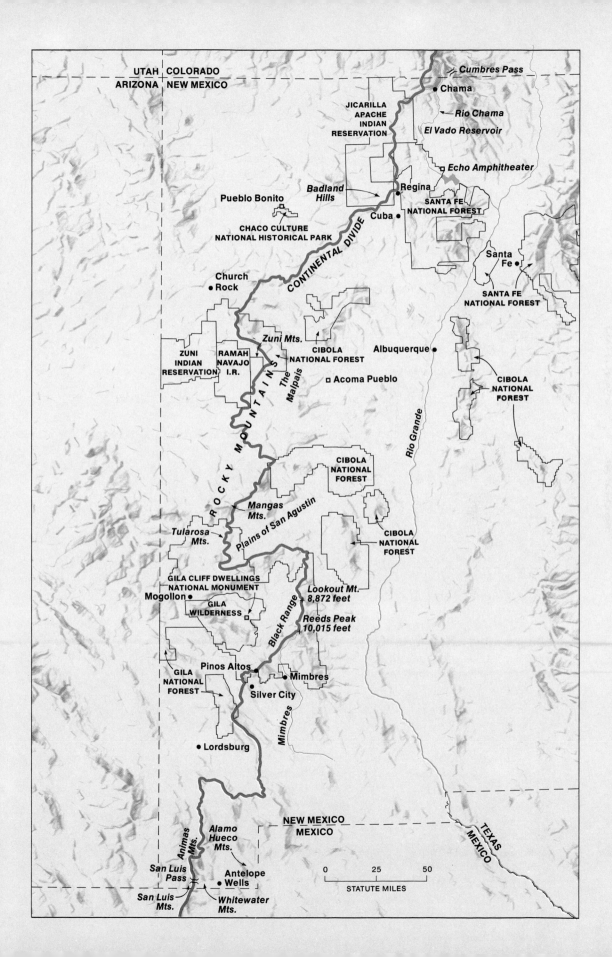

With the sun setting over San Luis Pass, author Mike Robbins turns his back on a fence that marks the border between the U.S. and Mexico. Earlier in the day, Mike crossed from Mexico at the lonely Antelope Wells border station (left). Customs inspector Ruby Madera-Font gives directions. "I used to be a customs officer in El Paso," she said, "but I wanted a quieter spot. I've found it." Ruby and her co-worker, the only two on duty here, live in house trailers behind the station.

Chef of the border, Mike concocts a "mostly Mexican" meal in honor of his proximity to the boundary. The ingredients: tortillas, refried beans, chilies, cheese, and tomatoes. The result: "Mexican pizza." Desert flora brightens his campsite. The cholla cactus (above and upper) bears red blossoms in spring and yellow fruit that may remain on the plant for several years. Coyotes eat the fruit, and the curve-billed thrasher nests in the plant. At right, prickly poppies bloom in a zone of desert grassland.

Whirling lariat and dodging calves recall the romance of the Old West in New Mexico. On the Culberson Ranch, cowboys Tom Day and Simon Arreola (far left) gather their gear for a day of roundup and branding. Simon, astride Piloto (above), lassos the skittish animals; at left, Tom brands them with the Culberson's registered mark: a Diamond-A. Ranching ranks as a vital industry in New Mexico, where cattle slightly outnumber people. Like men of an earlier day, Tom and Simon endure blustery winter chill and scorching summer sun to care for the herds.

Mountains. We walked in desert, recalling that at the border station Ruby had cautioned us about rattlesnakes. "I often see them in the cool of the mornings and evenings," she said.

We had a preconceived notion of "desert" as a place devoid of all wildlife except rattlers and rabbits, but as we reached the arid brown hills, oddly named the Whitewater Mountains, I spotted three coyotes loping toward a ridge. They went up and over without a pause, but they'd been eyeing us.

Soon after, on what our 1919 U.S. Geological Survey map (the most recent one available for the area) noted as the "R. I. Bass Ranch," we saw some wild pigs, not the small native peccaries, or javelinas, but something akin to wild boars, with dark coats and heavy snouts. They didn't look friendly. Through binoculars I watched one with a rusty red coat. His unblinking stare carried a message of such malevolence that I was glad we were beyond naked-eye proximity.

Hiking into the San Luis Mountains proved no easy matter. What our contour map suggested would be simple walking turned out to be slow stumbling over loose rocks and around cactus plants. There was no trail until we came onto a crude jeep road that the U.S. Border Patrol had bulldozed for access to one of the repeater stations that relay its radio signals. The patrol monitors the northbound traffic of illegal immigrants. Along likely roads, arroyos, and trails, hidden sensors can be set to record the vibrations of passing vehicles or pedestrians. The sensors are not an obstacle to crossing and smuggling, but the traffic at least is noted.

In midday warmth Paul and I rested at the repeater station. We broke out a light lunch of orange sections, cheddar cheese, raw carrots, trail mix, and plenty of water. Our 1,600-foot elevation above the floor of Animas Valley was sufficient for good views back into Mexico, where the gentle San Luis Mountains ascended to true mountain status; across to Animas Valley, where a wet spring had tinted wandering acres with the yellow of goldfield blossoms; and ahead to the ridges, where the hills converged upward across San Luis Pass into the Animas Mountains.

On San Luis Pass, at the end of a cloudless afternoon, the wind came up while we searched for a campsite. The best of the level ground was overgrown with dense clusters of man-size cholla cactus plants, many with arms tipped by waxy yellow fruit. The cholla taught us the value of an unexpectedly useful tool for desert camping: tweezers. Cholla spines are about an inch long, pale but springy and tough. Each has a barb at the end. Once embedded in a knee or elbow, the spine cannot be removed without breaking and further burying the barb. There it abscesses overnight, and what was merely an irritated speck in the evening becomes a very sore spot by morning. Luckily, Paul carried a pair of tweezers in his camera bag, and after our first encounter with the cholla, no barb was left untweezed.

When we set up our tent, we nearly lost it to the wind. We cooked in the wind, drifted to sleep in the wind, and awoke in the wind. Once it began rushing out of the west, it never let up. It brought a welcome dryness to our sweat-soaked shirts and packs, but it also carried dust from the adjacent valley, and peak gusts nearly bowled us over. Too, it brought pollutants from somewhere over the horizon, perhaps a smelter in Arizona or auto exhausts in distant cities. The air grew yellow and hazy around the sun and blue among the hills and mountain silhouettes.

Despite the dusty wind, we were determined to celebrate our closeness to the border with an approximately Mexican meal. Of course, we wouldn't always carry elaborate and heavy ingredients, but just for this one dinner. . . .

We unpacked flour tortillas, oil, fresh whole tomatoes, longhorn cheese, refried beans, and enchilada sauce with hot chilies. Prepared by his month-long camping trips with the National Outdoor Leadership School in Lander, Wyoming, Paul was our acknowledged master trail chef, but somehow it fell to me to prepare this first meal over the one-burner stove.

I heated oil in our light skillet, then flopped in a soft tortilla and gave it ample warm-up time. I applied slices of cheese, dollops of refried bean paste, segments of fresh tomato, and finally the enchilada sauce. The wind spiced it all with desert dust and cholla fragments until I covered the skillet and everything melted together. The outcome had more in common with pizza than with anything identifiably Mexican, but it was tasty and filling, and I cooked enough to satisfy the surprising appetites we'd worked up on this hot day.

By the time we had cleaned up after our dinner, darkness had fallen. Stars emerged and filled the sky in a profusion that belied any notion of air pollution. We stretched out on our foam pads, and Paul pointed out the constellations. I found the Big Dipper and Orion's Belt before sleep overtook me.

Once, deep in the night, I sat up and scanned the horizon. Around us the cholla loomed like otherworldly creatures and underscored our feelings of isolation. No light, no sign of human habitation could be seen. Nothing but wind and dark hills under the starlight. Borne to us on the constant wind, the nasal honks of cattle down in Animas Valley were a welcome sound, at times almost like voices.

After sunrise the Herefords were louder and closer. They were among thousands of cattle owned by the Gray Ranch Company. We had written to the resident manager for permission to hike and camp on the land, and also for information about the area. Gray Ranch encompasses in excess of 500 square miles, or about half of that area of New Mexico called the bootheel. All of the Animas Mountains lie within this one ranch, as do the first thirty miles of the Continental Divide in the United States. Ranch hands had told us that there was no water in the Animas Mountains, but that the well water for the stock tanks, pumped by the Gray's 68 windmills, was potable.

To learn more about water, trails, and desert wildlife, we stopped by a subranch of the Gray, the Culberson Ranch, occupied by Tom Day, his wife, Jerry, and a veteran hand, Simon Arreola. Fifty-four years on desert ranches had weathered Simon's face to a hue that matched the oak leaves still clinging to tough trees along the dry washes. He walked up from the corral where he'd been treating the hoof of a lamed saddle horse. He waved and said: "Have you any Spanish?"

When I shook my head, he laughed. "I have a leetle English." He held his thumb and forefinger about a quarter of an inch apart.

Tom was around on one side of the house digging a garden for Jerry, but he seemed happy to talk instead. He too was 54 years old and so exactly and unselfconsciously matched the image of a working rancher that he might have stepped directly from an advertisement to sunlit life. He was wearing dusty, scuffed cowboy boots, faded jeans, and a denim work shirt. He cupped a nonfilter cigarette between thumb and forefinger and regarded us from the shade of a tattered Stetson that curled perfectly from the sweat-stained junction of crown and brim. Tom listened with lively amusement in his eyes as we described our Continental Divide Trail project.

Tom and Simon have worked together since 1969 and are responsible for many of the ranching chores. I asked what that meant in terms of area and number of cattle. Tom squinted and figured. "About a hundred square miles, more or less. And maybe 1,500 head of cattle." Two hands in an area larger than the District of Columbia.

During the rest of a sparkling afternoon Paul and I sat on a corral fence and watched as Tom and Simon roped and branded some calves. One was a dogie, an orphaned calf that was being raised in a corral with a Guernsey milk cow.

Simon rode a pale horse named Piloto. He gave Piloto no more than a few exclamatory "clucks" and some knee pressure, but that was all the horse needed. Man and beast worked together as a unit, moving briskly around the corral after the first calf. Tom called out a suggestion to Simon that he rope it by the heels, something I'd have thought impossible. The calf skittered and dashed along the fence. Even after having seen it done, with an invisible flick of the wrist, I'm still inclined to say it's impossible.

Back in the ranch house for supper we got out our maps and asked about roads and trails closest to the Continental Divide. Like many residents we were to meet along the way, Tom wished he could drop what he was doing and hike along with us. "I used to walk a lot, cover a lot of ground fast. But," he shook his head, "these knees now...."

I asked about wildlife in the desert. Well, Tom told me, there are jackrabbits and cottontails and coyotes, of course. And javelinas. And, in a herd over in Animas Valley, a rare subspecies of pronghorn. And white-tailed and mule deer, "We don't permit hunting on the ranch anymore. I used to hunt deer, just for the food," Tom said. "But I don't like to kill them anymore. I just like to watch them."

We mentioned rattlesnakes. Tom smiled. "Two years ago I decided to keep the rattles of every snake we had to kill on the place, from spring to fall. Want to see them?" He left the room and soon returned with a half-gallon jar of rattles. He poured them out. "One hundred and five," he said.

To our surprise—and relief—we didn't see any rattlesnakes in the Animas Mountains or elsewhere in New Mexico. We learned, along the Divide, simply to be surprised by what we *did* see: by the brilliant green mesquite in the dry desert, by the narrow, daggerlike leaves of Spanish bayonet, by the immense golden eagle that swept low across our path, by the Swainson's hawk that allowed us to approach it.

On the vast flats north of the Animas Mountains, hiking the Divide became something less than an adventure: The problem was *finding* the Divide. Since there is little surface water to flow either east or west, the only way to locate the Divide is to use maps and a compass

Weathered buildings and mounds of tailings from the Fannie mine and mill cling to a slope of Fannie Hill near Mogollon. Beginning in the late 1880s, miners wrestled gold- and silver-bearing ore up the mine's 1,100-foot shaft.

FOLLOWING PAGES: *Slanting rays of sunlight gild a bajada—an area of rippling hills built of wash from nearby uplands.*

Very Large Array—the world's biggest and most powerful radio telescope—turns sensitive ears toward deep space on the Plains of San Agustin. The 27 antennas, their signals combined and strengthened by computer, can perform as one giant instrument.

to check the directions of the dry washes. The flat zone southeast of Silver City is one of only two known places along the Divide where the water doesn't divide but instead goes into a kind of hydrologic "black hole." It simply disappears underground.

Above Silver City, a freshly booming old-time mining town and supply center for miners and hikers, the Continental Divide bulges eastward to trace the peaks and ridgelines of the rugged Black Range. For some sixty miles the trail coincides with the Divide. Many hikers going the full distance to Canada have been striking straight north from Silver City to traverse the better watered and more scenic Gila Wilderness and to stop over at Sapillo Creek and Gila Cliff Dwellings

National Monument. We tried both ways, first hiking sections of the trail in the Black Range, then exploring the cliff dwellings and the Gila Wilderness.

The trail around Silver City is in excellent shape, thanks to some volunteer trailblazers. "We're clearing the trail so the greenest greenhorn can follow it without getting lost, on foot or on horseback." Rita Hotchkiss thus described the work she and her husband, Rufe, had done in clearing and marking Continental Divide trail near their Silver City ranch. "Back in the 1930s the CCC had a camp near here and laid out a trail along the Divide from Pinos Altos to Mimbres. In fifty years, though, a lot of brush grows up. The old ax marks get grown over. Trees with blazes die or get burned. Rufe found the old trail and worked it out, and we've been clearing now for about eight years." Rita is in her 60s and Rufe is over 70.

We hiked sections of trail cleared by the Hotchkisses between Chloride Flat and an old homestead near Black Peak. With brush and boulders removed, branches trimmed high and wide for packhorses, and easily seen blazes, it was some of the best trail we hiked.

In the Black Range, trails became problematical. Along the spine of the mountains at about 8,000 feet the pine forest is clear, mostly ponderosa, with light gravel and dry needles underfoot. Except for the scarcity of drinking water—there is only one spring on the main trail from Reeds Peak to Lookout Mountain, a two-day stint—this is good hiking country. It is easy walking but hard navigating.

"The secondary trails in this section of the Black Range have not really been maintained for about ten years," Cindy Waddell told me. Cindy is one of the two lookouts at the forest service tower on 8,872-foot Lookout Mountain. On the morning I came by to ask for directions, she was busy with binoculars, firefinder, and radio. The vigorous lightning storm that rumbled and flashed overhead—and that had awakened me repeatedly during the previous night—had touched off at least fifty fires in the Gila National Forest. One blaze was smoking and flaring only six miles away on a nameless peak above Doubtful Canyon. It was in a heavy fuel area and a strong wind was blowing, so Cindy called the dispatcher, who sent smoke jumpers and a slurry bomber from Silver City. We watched as the jumper plane circled and dropped two silver parachutes that drifted down into the thick pines west of the fire. Cindy talked by radio with the pilots and the base as the slurry bomber, a World War II B-17, took its turn and made a slow flight through the twisting smoke and—at what looked like treetop level—spewed a shower of ruby-red fire retardant in the path of the blaze. Between radio questions and answers, Cindy talked about the trails.

"I once went to hike down to Monument Park, about two miles to the south. You can even see it from here," she said. I looked and picked out the cabin in the ponderosas, its roof painted the same green as the roof planks in sets of toy Lincoln logs. "There's a trail sign pointing to it, with the mileage marked and everything. But in three-quarters of a mile that trail just petered out. I had to go cross-country."

North of the lookout I lost and found the trail several times. I started toward Franks Mountain at the end of the Black Range and the beginning of the Plains of San Agustin. A new sign read "Forest Trail" and pointed north. But the arrow seemed to lead to a single marked tree and no more. I circled and studied likely old trees, remembering Rita Hotchkiss's comment about her husband, Rufe: "He's a wizard at spotting old blazes." Finally, I stopped for lunch and considered my want of such wizardry.

The *idea* of a trail is so compelling and the black lines so unambiguous on the maps that it is hard to accept the possibility of not even finding the trail. But the actual mountains and forests are vast, and where a map shows a single line there may be many trails, old and new, human and game. There may be logging roads, rights-of-way, old blazes for fence builders, cattle trails. The very idea of a single, clear path begins to seem questionable.

While in the Black Range, Paul and I spotted the tracks of turkeys, elk, bobcats, and mountain lions. Once we flushed a mother turkey. Her young brown brood exploded into flight in all directions. Later we glimpsed a glossy black bear in a green clearing. But we also learned that there was more to watch for along the Divide than trail blazes and animal signs. Gila National Forest Ranger Ron Bradsby told us he'd recently caught several pothunters as they were looting prehistoric Indian sites.

Standing where the Mimbres River flows parallel to the Continental Divide ridges, Ron gestured toward the riverside bluffs. "Nearly all these breaks have some kind of habitation site on top. Pithouses, mostly. There's not much above ground, just some rocks. But after a while you get so you can pick them out."

Earlier in his office Ron had shown Paul and me a map of sites occupied along the Mimbres River and the Continental Divide by Mimbres Indians, a people of the Mogollon Culture. They occupied the Mimbres drainage, which is peppered with sites, until about A.D. 1130. It was the custom of the Mimbrenos to bury their dead under the floors of their dwellings along with their possessions, which usually included pottery.

It is this classic black-on-white ware that the pothunters sought. It is decorated with finely executed images of birds, fish, insects, and larger animals, as well as the Mimbrenos fishing, fighting, and farming — scenes from their daily lives. Often mythological beasts and stories are intertwined with the realistic images.

We climbed from the river up through the piñons to a level blufftop. Ron found a clearing and pointed. "There's a pithouse site." It was a rough rectangle of flat stones, each about the size of a shoebox, arranged around a shallow depression. I could see that it differed from the natural surroundings, that *something* had been done here by humans. "This one was probably inhabited about a thousand years ago," Ron said. "And it's never been excavated."

Across the Divide we hiked to a site where nearly an acre of pithouse sites, a whole village, had been looted by pothunters. As we crossed mounds of thrown-up earth, something very white caught my eye. I stirred the dust with my boot. It was a vertebra, one perfect section of a human backbone, perhaps a thousand years old. I tried to remember if I'd ever before found a human bone.

Such places were more peopled, and perhaps more civilized, in millennia past than they are in our time. Two—Gila Cliff Dwellings National Monument and Chaco Culture National Historical Park—are short detours from the Continental Divide.

We chanced to arrive at Gila on Memorial Day weekend. The people who were there on holiday filled the campground with tents and recreational vehicles. The people who had lived there 700 years earlier had built a community in six caves 175 feet above the canyon floor. These were Mogollon people (our name; we don't know what they called themselves), some of whom were probably the ancestors of modern-day Pueblo Indians. About a dozen families evidently lived and worked and played in these forty stone rooms. They went down and out to hunt and to gather edible plants and to raise maize and beans and squash. They climbed back up to cook and eat and sleep. Theirs must have been a close, noisy life.

We walked through their rooms, stooping at doorways. We were reminded of childhood forts, anthills, fishing villages, funhouses—places of liveliness. These people wore cotton clothes, sandals, and headbands. They used bows and arrows and made clay vessels. The clothes, tools, weapons, pots, and stone metates they left behind when they — like nearly all the peoples of the Southwest — went away somewhere in the mid-1300s, have been gathered for preservation and study in such places as the Museum of New Mexico's Laboratory of Anthropology in Santa Fe and the Maxwell Museum at the University of New Mexico in Albuquerque: centers of civilization.

Chaco Canyon is overwhelming. It's out of the way now, a dusty-road side trip, but once down in the canyon and among the acres of complex ruins, you understand that this was a center. The canyon itself, cut by the occasionally flowing Chaco Wash, is less than a mile wide. The national monument occupies a strip about 12 miles long, and in that area are at least 13 major ruins and thousands of archaeological sites. This is the home ground of peoples ranging from Pleistocene hunters to modern Navajos. "Ruins" seems an inexact term for sandstone buildings that over the centuries housed thousands of people and are still standing four stories tall.

The buildings are mostly the work of a people today's Navajo call the Anasazi. They lived here from about the start of the Christian era until 1300 or so and reached a peak in the 11th and 12th centuries. They designed and constructed towns, water-control systems, and networks of roads. Some 1,200 inhabitants raised crops, traded in turquoise, copper bells, and parrots, and evidently lived a ceremonious life with special buildings, costumes, art, music, and ornament. If recent findings about the arrangement of stones atop Fajada Butte are correct, they also studied and understood something of the stars.

We lingered longest at Pueblo Bonito, an elaborately planned community, an 800-room hive of connected living spaces. As we stepped from room to room, we felt that music should be playing to underscore the air of order and harmony. Vents for windows, wooden roofs, plazas, veneered masonry—this is *architecture*. These were people of successful community organization, of engineering talent and specialization, of aesthetic sensitivity and vision. It is easy to imagine living here.

Although we had detoured to see the surviving ancient Indian communities, no detour was necessary to encounter present-day Indians. Indeed, the Continental Divide in New Mexico crosses the reservations of the Ramah Navajo and the Jicarilla Apache and passes near the Zuni and Acoma reservations as well. No hiking trails or facilities are developed on these lands. They are sparsely populated and, except for sheep herding, not intensely used. Tribal representatives made it clear that trespassers are not welcome, but hikers who request permission in advance are permitted on reservation lands.

At Pine Hill, on the Ramah Navajo Indian Reservation, Paul and I met with Bennie Cohoe, chapter president — "like a community mayor" — of the 230 square miles and 1,600 residents of Ramah. Bennie is a bespectacled, muscular bundle of energy and ideas whose ranch is at Sierra Alto, in sight of the Continental Divide. He heads several of the organizations that have transformed life in the Ramah community in the past decade. He set up craft classes so that the people who had retained rare traditional skills could teach them to a new generation.

One hot, hushed afternoon we looked in on a white-walled hogan where Annie Chatto, in a full purple skirt and rimless glasses, was making baskets along with Winora Pino and Mable Alonzo. They were using shaved willow strips they'd gathered near Quemado, fifty miles away, to weave water jugs and ceremonial wedding baskets. The jugs would be coated with melted pine pitch that would dry to dark brown. Marty Garcia, Bennie Cohoe's assistant and the only member of the influential Ramah Navajo School Board who speaks fluent English, explained: "There was a time not long ago when the only baskets around were very old ones. No one was making them."

The baskets are ceremonial and important, woven in a red and black pattern of five points near the center and twelve points around the margin. The pattern always incorporates a break, an opening in the geometry of colors, and when in use the opening—like the door of every Navajo hogan—must face toward the east, the source of each new day. Making these baskets is a tradition that was caught on the brink of extinction. Annie Chatto is one who remembers the old skills and is passing them on.

Weaving rugs of the wool from their sheep is a Navajo tradition that has survived with unbroken vigor. At ranches and outside scattered hogans we watched Navajo women at their looms. The emergent rugs were familiar, of course, in the blacks, grays, and reds, the balanced patterns that are seen in museums, galleries, and shops. Nothing else seemed familiar. No one spoke English. There were no

Ageless at 80, and as timeless as the intricate rugs she weaves, Minnie Martine still helps tend the flocks of sheep that sustain Navajos on their Ramah reservation in western New Mexico.

Danny Lee, an 18-year-old Navajo, drives a flock of sheep to pasture near Church Rock. At left, he leaves his six-sided hogan, where his aunt Nellie Mae Davis weaves. Behind a loom laced with threads (far left), Nellie cradles her grandson. Her deft fingers will turn the fibers into a rug like the one below.

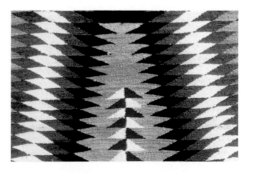

47

telephones and no electric power. We were not simply on private land; we were on the home ground of another culture, another tradition. Standing at a screen of juniper branches in the smoke drifting from a charcoal fire that discouraged the worst of the gnats, and watching a woman weave an intricate rug in patterned shades of brown on an ageless wooden loom, I had to remind myself that we stood within the bounds of the United States in the late 20th century.

Alice Alonzo is a famous weaver. She had shorn this wool from her own sheep, then colored it in vegetable dyes she had made in her kitchen. The loom in her front room was wooden, a vertical frame of two-by-six timbers. It held part of a rug three feet by five feet in a pattern of two different grays, one black, one white, and one red, all in a tight zigzag. The house was full of people—children, teen-age girls, rowdy boys, older ones—and scrawny dogs and wily cats. Alice ignored everything and said nothing as she worked the loom, repeating the practiced motions. I could not calculate her age. Her black hair was parted across the exact center of her head. She wore turquoise earrings, a full skirt, and a plaid blouse. It had taken her three weeks to weave the two feet of rug on the loom. She would receive several hundred dollars for the completed rug. With Marty Garcia translating, I asked a question. Marty nodded back at me. Yes, Alice has been doing this all her life.

On a corner of the Jicarilla reservation in the fading light of a lavender evening, Paul and I wandered among the scarred hogbacks and arroyos and across the colored clay plains of a region called the Badland Hills, astride the Continental Divide.

"This is just the kind of area where you'll find an arrowhead," Paul said.

"Projectile point," I said, but kept looking.

We'd been looking at the earth anyway, wishing the light would last. This is a peculiar area of violet clay cliffs, standing rocks that are crumbling to sand, and caves and "windows" in the cliffs that house restless birds. Scattered in eroded clefts and alluvial fans were bones, fossils, and what seemed to be petrified wood—puzzle pieces from other ages. Paul stopped.

"There," he said, and stooped to examine a point, an inch and a half of wedge-shaped translucent white quartz that had been chipped at the edges. It was spare and sharp and beautiful, and we laughed in astonishment and pleasure.

Paul's find left us eager for more days in this region, which stretches from just northwest of Cuba to the lakes west of Chama. It is a range of hills unlike any we'd seen, a mysterious, empty miniature of the terrain that characterizes much of New Mexico: striated cliffs and buttes of warm and improbable colors.

The Badland Hills region has trails made by animals, men, and machines. There are old roads to follow, hunter tracks, blazes along the ridgetops, and game traces. I was following one such trace, hiking north along a butte in sight of the town of Regina. Years before, someone had blazed this trail, mostly following the lead of the deer, and had cut rectangles on the piñon and juniper trunks. The trail was

48

faint, and as often as not I followed the line of least resistance among the shrubs and sandstone boulders. I was within earshot of a valley sawmill and within sight of Hatch Lake and Route 96.

Hiking uphill atop the eastside cliffs, I paused for a swallow of water in a level clay area that had eroded along one side to form a sandy patch about six feet across. In the middle on the surface I spotted a potsherd the size of my hand. It was gently curved, plain brown, and less than a quarter of an inch thick. It was slipped and scored, much like the thousand-year-old pots I had seen in the museum in Santa Fe. There was another sherd, and another, different colors and curves. Standing still, I scanned the entire area around my feet and realized I was standing on a familiar rough rectangle of stones surrounding a slight depression, a zone of disturbed earth. It was a pithouse site—never looted, never excavated. I circled. Along the ridgetop there was another pithouse, and another. I had walked onto a small village of ruins in plain sight of a highway but never touched. I examined the clay and rocks and flapped a spare shirt at the gnats. Eventually, I spied some stone tools made of a hard white rock: among them, a scraper, and another that felt like a punch or an awl. I remembered what forest service archaeologist Steve Sigstad had told me about identifying ancient tools: "They've been worked, and they fit your hand." I closed my hand. They fit.

As we approached the New Mexico-Colorado border, we took advantage of two opportunities to see the country along the Continental Divide from other-than-pedestrian viewpoints: from a river raft and from a railroad car.

The Rio Chama flows parallel to the Divide. It is dammed to form El Vado Reservoir, and below the reservoir in the Santa Fe National Forest the river winds among cliffs and meadows. During spring floods, an exciting white-water raft passage is possible through country that is far from any road or trail. We floated along with white-water guide and anthropologist Steve Miller of Santa Fe on the maiden voyage of his raft. Steve is a born teacher who read the river aloud as we shifted among the rocks and vortices. First, we would hear the roar of the water ahead, then we would experience long, exhilarating moments as we plunged into standing waves that doused us from head to foot. The cold water froze our breath. At times, manning one of the forward paddles, I would lose sight of Paul at the other paddle when the water sluiced over us.

There were long stretches of calm river too, when mergansers would start from the willowed banks and swallows swarm from the pocked cliffs overhead. During one of those placid intervals a long thick snake swam in shimmering (Continued on page 54)

FOLLOWING PAGES: *Like an island in the sky, Acoma stands on a seventy-acre tabletop. For a thousand years, Pueblo Indians have lived here. They once descended the cliffs by precarious trails to their farms; now a road reaches the settlement. Under Spanish rule, they carried earth and timbers to the top in the 1600s to build the massive Roman Catholic church and its cemetery.*

W ater etches the
Badland Hills. A
maze of cracks (above),
formed when mud dried
and shrank, surrounds a
short-horned lizard. At
left, Mike climbs where
seasonal downpours
have gullied soft clay.
Another climber
encourages him from the
summit. "Climbing the
slippery surface is
tricky," says Mike, "and
if you dig your foot in,
the clay crumbles."

angles just under the surface directly before us. It seemed propelled from some outside source, shot along in the rippled water. No one could get a clear enough look at the colors and markings to identify it. Upstream, on the pebbled shore, it slithered among the grass clumps and disappeared.

The town of Chama, on the river of the same name, is locally renowned for another water creature: trout. The river rushes down from the snowfields of the San Juan Mountains, and rainbow, brown, and cutthroat trout flourish in the cold waters. Chama is more than 8,000 feet high, and around it the high country snows define the seasons. Fishermen begin arriving in late June, the trout catch peaks in mid-July, and by late October the high passes are closing under early winter. The snows also limit the operating season of the Cumbres and Toltec Scenic Railroad.

Since 1881 people—mostly miners and loggers—and freight have traveled from Chama across the Colorado border on the three-foot-gauge tracks of the Denver and Rio Grande Railway. Sixty-four miles of the San Juan Extension, together with steam engines, rotary snowplows, freight cars, stations, and yards, have been purchased by Colorado and New Mexico and now operate as an excursion line. Two trains a day run during the snow-free months. We decided that a day's ride up over 10,022-foot Cumbres Pass in Colorado would be an effortless introduction to the serious high country along the Divide.

Shortly after breakfast we found the coal-fired 1925 Baldwin locomotive already steaming and sending a pungent column of smoke breezing toward the morning sun. About 150 passengers boarded the cars and we started up what conductor Richard Braden described as the toughest railroad grade in North America: 4 percent for 14 miles.

On this climb, 12 cars at 12 miles an hour were all that could be managed by the single engine. Up ahead, it puffed and whistled. As we brushed through the thick pines and snow-bent, restless aspens at trackside, the engine sent clouds of grit-bearing coal smoke wafting back through the cars. No one appeared to mind.

In the last car, an open gondola lined with photographers, the sun grew hot over the cool mountain wind. Alongside, in the high meadows and valleys, water was rushing everywhere. We began to cross its sources in dirty drifts of snow. We passed crashing streams, reflective pools, beaver ponds, and sopping meadows. The grass was lush in the intense green of late spring and punctuated by sprouts of skunk cabbage. Dandelion blossoms spread a yellow haze alongside. The chuffing engine and the rumbling, clattering cars were not about to sneak up on any wildlife, but beavers and marmots stared back at us. Through the uphill stands of pine we caught glimpses of mule deer. As we climbed near Cumbres Pass, we could see rising to the north mountains higher than any we had yet encountered: the Colorado San Juans, peaks still draped in snow.

Russet sandstone walls rise above campers in Echo Amphitheater. "Spooky by night, spectacular by day," says Mike of the formation.

With an overturned kayaker in his wake, white-water guide Steve Miller

At STONY PASS, under a summer sun, I slipped out of my pack and knelt with a water bottle on the moist dark earth beside a soiled snowbank. I wedged the bottle flat against the ground and waited with my thirst while cold snowmelt trickled in. Here was the beginning of the mighty Rio Grande, and I was diverting its entire flow into a plastic bottle.

In the San Juan Mountains of Colorado we found the Continental Divide's true mountain country, with its surprising, insistent, and hazardous weather; its visible, vital divisions of the waters; its mineral wealth; its winter world and the wildlife that has adapted to it. Here, in Colorado, we would learn about the high country.

Paul and I hiked and explored several sections of the Divide in the San Juans, where many volcanic peaks exceed 13,000 feet, and the passes are higher than 10,000 feet. Much of the terrain is above timberline. It is a spare and windy land once roamed by prehistoric hunters and historic miners and now worked by geologists, outfitters, fishermen, hunters, skiers, and sheepherders.

The Divide enters Colorado from New Mexico on private land but thereafter, except for a few miles, is entirely in national forests or in Rocky Mountain National Park. It bisects the state, and here, more than in most places, it is a definite barrier to land travel and a divider of economies and life-styles.

From the old mining town of Summitville, the Divide swings west toward Silverton in a long loop around the volcanic caldera at Creede and the valley of the Rio Grande. Then it turns east and north toward Salida and the Collegiate Peaks, with their clustered array of "fourteeners"—mountains more than 14,000 feet high. Just east of the Divide at Independence Pass is Mount Elbert, at 14,433 feet the highest in Colorado. The Divide half circles Leadville in mountains where every acre has been prospected, if not actually mined, for gold, silver, lead, zinc, and molybdenum. Then it points north, defining Colorado's famous ski resorts. In Rocky Mountain Park it turns slightly west. As it leaves the park, it dips south along the Never Summer Mountains and then runs directly west. Near the ski mecca of Steamboat Springs, the Divide heads north through the Mount Zirkel Wilderness and, at about 10,000 feet, passes into Wyoming.

Through much of the national forests, and also in Rocky Mountain National Park, a number of good hiking trails already exist on or near the Divide. In the loop around the Rio Grande Valley, a route long known as the Continental Divide Trail all but coincides with the Divide. There are other established, useful trails, such as the Timberline Trail in the Gunnison National Forest, the High Lonesome Trail in the Arapaho National Forest, and the Colorado Trail—the old Main Range Trail—in the San Isabel National Forest. But it was here in the mountains of Colorado that we first realized the physiographic and

Flanked almost entirely by federal lands, the Divide in the U.S. climbs to its highest elevations in Colorado. The Rio Grande, Colorado, and other major rivers arise here, in high country studded with old and new mines, ghost towns, and celebrated ski resorts.

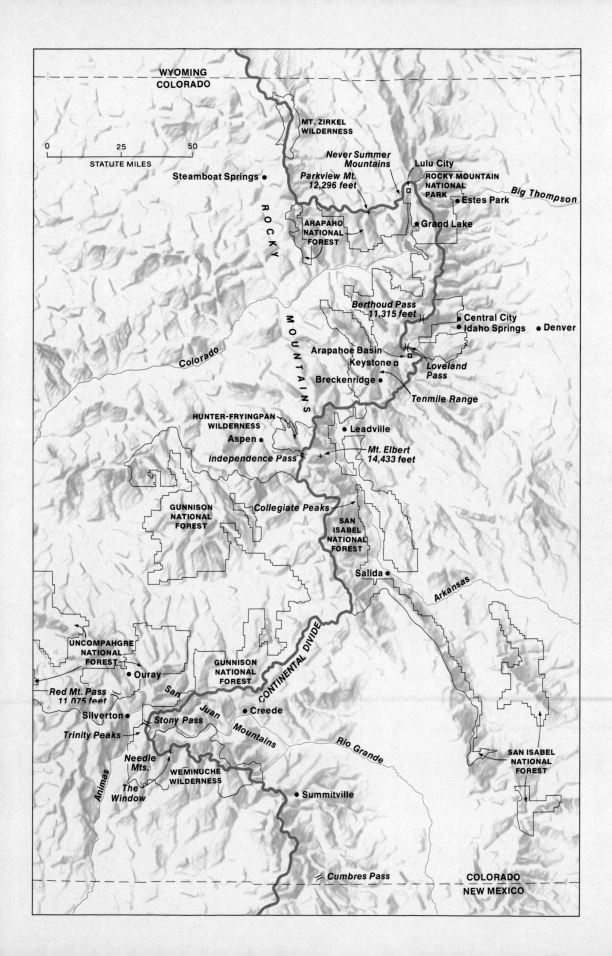

WYOMING
COLORADO

0   25   50
STATUTE MILES

MT. ZIRKEL
WILDERNESS

Never Summer Mountains

Lulu City

Steamboat Springs •

*Parkview Mt.
12,296 feet*

ROCKY MOUNTAIN
NATIONAL
PARK

• Estes Park

Big Thompson

R
O
C
K
Y

ARAPAHO
NATIONAL
FOREST

• Grand Lake

*Berthoud Pass
11,315 feet*

• Central City
• Idaho Springs

• Denver

M
O
U
N
T
A
I
N
S

Colorado

Arapahoe Basin
Keystone □

*Loveland
Pass*

• Breckenridge

Tenmile Range

HUNTER-FRYINGPAN
WILDERNESS

• Leadville

Aspen •

*Mt. Elbert
14,433 feet*

Independence Pass

GUNNISON
NATIONAL
FOREST

Collegiate Peaks

SAN
ISABEL
NATIONAL
FOREST

• Salida

Arkansas

UNCOMPAHGRE
NATIONAL
FOREST

GUNNISON
NATIONAL
FOREST

C
O
N
T
I
N
E
N
T
A
L

D
I
V
I
D
E

• Ouray

*Red Mt. Pass
11,075 feet*

San

Silverton •

Stony Pass

Juan

• Creede

Trinity Peaks

Mountains

Rio Grande

SAN ISABEL
NATIONAL
FOREST

*Needle
Mts.*

WEMINUCHE
WILDERNESS

Animas

*The
Window*

• Summitville

Cumbres Pass

COLORADO
NEW MEXICO

The Window—a ridgetop landmark (left)—gapes in the Divide beyond campers in Colorado's Weminuche Wilderness. Bad weather foiled Mike and his companions' hopes for a panoramic view westward through the Window. Dense fog (opposite) shrouds the opening. Below, wrangler Chris Broyles, Mike, and trip leader Ken Ellison escape the drizzle under an outcropping directly on the Divide.

climatic impracticality of hiking directly on the Continental Divide.

We hadn't expected a snowfall during an August horse-pack trip. When we reined to a halt on the narrow 12,857-foot-high ledge of *La Ventana*—the Window—snow flurries swirled out of the freezing fog. Outfitter Ken Ellison, his son Eric, a wrangler from Texas named Chris Broyles, and Paul and I, had taken most of the morning to guide our horses up from our camp in the Weminuche Wilderness. We sought the long view west into the Needle Mountains, the tight, high peaks rising above the Animas River, and into the deep valleys. But a floor of dirty clouds was gliding directly into us, running through the gaps and passes, reducing visibility from miles to yards. Then heavier snow furled around us and we could see even less.

The Window is a landmark, a geometric notch about 150 feet high. It was named by Spanish gold miners in the 18th century, and from a distance it is as distinct as a missing tooth. We waited, disappointed, in the blowing fog, gusty showers, and snow. Occasionally the thick clouds would drift away from the mountainsides, and we could see the green gulch of East Ute Creek below.

There was just enough room for us on the sloping ledge, and our horses stirred nervously on the pale, brittle gravel. Finally, growing wetter and colder, we gave up and turned back toward camp.

It had been a tense, steep ascent to the Window. There were game trails among the stunted willows, and we switchbacked every few yards. But as the slope grew steeper, the turns got trickier for the horses. My mount—a young white mare named Dilly—had repeatedly stumbled, puffed, and otherwise demonstrated her want of agility during the long trail ride. Ken explained that Dilly was a bit out of shape: She had escaped from her pasture and spent several gluttonous weeks in the bottoms along the Rio Grande. Dilly lunged in the steep uphill turns, and I knew that if she stumbled and went down, we would be tangled in a long, damaging fall.

Back at our tents, under a bitter rain, we discovered one of the happy differences between backpacking and horse-packing. Ken's trail cook, Lesli, had put together a sumptuous hot meal: panfried chicken and fresh, warm biscuits, a tossed salad, hot coffee, and baked brownies for dessert. We crowded gratefully into the sheepherder tent that was being kept warm and dry by a wood stove.

Ken Ellison's usual business—and that of many ranchers in the San Juans—is guiding and outfitting fishermen and elk hunters. These mountains are a major habitat along the Divide for *Cervus canadensis*—the North American elk, or wapiti. Some 10,000 of the animals summer along the Divide, feeding on grasses and shrubs. After their rambunctious rutting in September, they move down from the Divide on migrations that take them through the aspen, which elk enjoy gnawing. About that time, the elk-hunting season opens.

For 22 days, some 3,500 armed men camp in and roam through the mountains, and in an average year they kill 600 elk. I'm not a hunter, and have never felt the urge to kill an animal; perhaps I've never been hungry enough. "A hunter is a harvester, that's the way I look at it," Glen Hinshaw told me. He is Colorado's district wildlife manager in the San Juans, and his no-nonsense demeanor must be well known to the hundreds of elk hunters who return here year after year. "If we allowed the big game animals to breed unharvested, they would overpopulate an area, then die off. That's what I think is immoral: to let that protein rot into the ground. Six hundred elk harvested each year translates into 60,000 pounds of processed meat in the freezer."

The elk, which had largely disappeared by 1900, have been reintroduced and are now increasing in number, largely because of the controlled hunting, Glen says. Other causes of death among elk: old age, disease, and road kills. "But the major threat to the well-being of the elk is loss of suitable habitat," Glen continued. "They need quality forage and good winter range." And that habitat is being lost to farming, ranching, and especially to various kinds of development.

Hunting is one of those activities that persist long after their original basis for being has eroded. It has become a sport. Hunting is one such activity, and we encountered others along the Divide: fishing, steam railroading, skiing, backpacking itself, and dogsledding.

In Europe and North America, generations of hardy dogs have been bred to perform burdensome work, often in snow. Nowadays, in North America at least, they rarely work. Instead, they race. Siberian huskies, like the ones bred, raised, shown, and raced by J. W. and Joan Campbell of Gunnison, are testimony to the success of selective breeding. All the dogs want to do is get going. They're so keen to hit the trail, at a dead run, that it's impossible to harness more than one without first tying the sled to a tree. Otherwise the first dogs in harness will simply take off.

For a dogsled camping trip in the San Juans, Paul and I rendezvoused with the Campbells and their Siberians on Red Mountain Pass near Ouray. The dawn light intensified from a lavender wash to brilliant silver as we stowed our gear on the laminated-wood sleds. The excited dogs leaped, howled, and yapped as J. W. hitched eight of them to his sled and four to the lighter sled I was to use.

"The first rule of dogsledding," J. W. explained, "is never let go of the sled—no matter what happens. If you do, you may have to hike five miles to catch up with it." He showed me the brake, a spring-loaded, hinged wooden bar that the driver presses down into the snow to stop. J. W. said: "If you put your full weight on the brake and shout 'Whoa!' or 'Ho!' or 'No!' at the top of your lungs, the dogs will at least slow down—if they feel like it." J. W. then introduced me to my team: two females named Muki and Davyet, and two males, Arty and Glacier. Arty was to prove strong and lovable but unruly. He had a gift for tangling himself and the others in his harness.

The sun came over the mountain into a cloudless sky, and we were ready to go. J. W. untied my sled first, and, freed at last, the happy Siberians stopped barking and shot (Continued on page 70)

FOLLOWING PAGES: *Crumpled ranks of the Needle Mountains march westward from the Divide. Sunlight Peak rises at left, beyond lakes stocked by the state of Colorado with cutthroat trout.*

Husky power provides Mike with a tour of Red Mountain Pass in the San Juan Mountains. At left, he "pedals" during an uphill stretch. Day's work done, J. W. Campbell (below), who raises the dogs for racing and showing, shares an affectionate moment with Red Mittens. At right, J. W.'s wife, Joan, transfers pups Mittens and Igloo from the gangline to their overnight stakeout chain.

FOLLOWING PAGES: *Awakening to three inches of new April snow, Mike and J.W. prepare the morning coffee. Of the tiny tree near their fire, J. W. says: "In summer, after the snow melts, it will probably show up as an 8-to-10-foot beauty."*

forward. The narrow sled teetered and skidded across the deep, bumpy snow. I crouched at the back, holding onto the curved wooden bar, and tried to keep my footing on the two thin runners. J. W. and his team were right behind us as we flew along the sparkling snow past shadowy islands of dark pines. I kept the sled upright and in hand until we approached a sharp drop-off. I turned to see how J. W. would handle it, and wanted to ask what to do, but there was no time. The Siberians didn't hesitate; they plunged over the crest.

For a few moments they stayed ahead of me on my careening sled. Then Muki floundered, and Arty lost his footing and somersaulted. I parted from the overturning sled, and we all descended together in a lunging, flying tangle of lines, dogs, packs, and swirling snow. At the bottom of the hill, half under the upside-down sled, I learned that even snarled harnesses, dragging cargo, and unsledded rider present no serious hindrance to the Siberians' pulling power. They continued straight ahead until I got untangled and upright, and—shouting "Whoa! Whoa!"—fell on the brake.

J. W. and his team chose a more gradual, prudent angle of descent. With Paul and Joan he soon caught up, all of them shaking with laughter. "I've never seen the dogs take a hill like that," J. W. said. "Usually they have better sense."

In late afternoon we sledded onto a level campsite on a partly wooded bluff between two ridges. The sky had gradually clouded over during the afternoon, and by the time we began staking out the dogs and setting up our tents, the first flakes were blowing around us. Hitched to a long, substantial chain, the Siberians clamored until fed. Then they quieted, ignored the growing storm, and curled up to sleep in the snow, their plumed tails muffling their noses.

It was snowing hard by the time we got the tents up and secured against the wind. One winter-camping caution was soon obvious: Get all the gear inside during a snowstorm, lest it be buried and hidden until spring. Fumbling in gloved hands, I took at least three times longer than usual to make hot chocolate, coffee, and dinner. We ate quickly in the fading light, backs to the driving snow and hands cupping our hot dinner bowls. After a hasty cleanup, I checked my tent lines and crawled inside to early darkness.

I had two battery-powered lights and used them both while arranging my gear in the tent. Once settled, I lighted a small candle in a miniature aluminum lantern. It drooled warm wax onto the tent floor, but its appearance of warmth was welcome.

Lying alone in the tent during the snowstorm, I listened as the wind moaned and shrilled in the trees. The tent walls rippled and bellied. The flying snow hissed around the tent. I was aware—as if I were hovering overhead—of our location on the mountain, aware of the drifting snow and the rocky outcrops, the twisting trees and the blackness of the night. I saw our improbably colored tents perched like two bright beads on a vast frozen plateau.

Like the extreme weather, mining is an inescapable presence along the Continental Divide in Colorado. Extraction of gold, silver, and other minerals has been a shaper of life in the Rockies for more than a century. In the San Juans and the ranges of central Colorado, a hiker often sees the evidence of mining: portals, mine dumps, shaft houses, mills, and aerial tramways. The promise of fortunes spurred men to perform engineering miracles at these high elevations, and when they were finished, whether the promise was kept or broken, they walked away from the hardware.

The aerial tramways caught my eye and made me curious about mining. Around Silverton and Ouray we had seen the long lines looping thousands of feet down from peaks above timberline to the valley floors. From small mines up among the eagles, these cables had floated iron buckets of heavy ore supplies, and even men, over impassably steep and rugged terrain to the processing mills below. From cables long out of use, the buckets still hung swaying in the wind.

In 1859 John H. Gregory was the first to strike lode gold in Colorado. The ensuing boom created the legendary Central City—part of what has been called the richest square mile on earth. I met the mayor of Central City, Bill Russell, conducting business over strong coffee. A gaunt, tall man with energetic eyes, Bill owns 800 acres of mining property and seems a personification of mining's lure: "My great-grandfather was a forty-niner," he told me. "My grandfather was a 'fifty-niner' at the Comstock Lode in Nevada. My father was a sour-dough who went to the Klondike in the 1890s. I started working the mines in this area in 1937."

That was long after the bonanza days. Contrary to popular myth, miners didn't always quit "because the color played out." Often the mines were shut down with gold and silver still present, but, for one reason or another, extracting the minerals had become unprofitable. But the mine that was a heartbreaking loser when gold sold for $20 an ounce is a different story when it's hundreds of dollars an ounce.

"The price of gold has caused a lot of interest," Bill said. "Lots of people coming up here, trespassing on creeks to pan gold—they don't realize that the mine claims include the creeks. That's stealing—what we call 'high-grading'—and people get shot for doing it." He laughed. "Flatlanders think these are all abandoned mines, just 'cause they aren't being worked just now. Hell, I pay taxes on mine. I don't know how people figure they're abandoned."

I asked whether there was a renewal of serious mining in this historic district. Bill began naming mines that were active: the Gold Ridge, the Togo, the Two Brothers, the Peru. "It's hard and expensive to reopen a mine. You've got to clean it all out, clean the portal up," he said. "You've got to dig a tunnel, and scrape off the dump for a building site. Then timber in for maybe thirty feet until you get to solid rock. You've got to run railroad track in, and that's expensive." He remembered that the Jack Pine Mining Company was opening several old mines and sent me to its president, Doug Watrous.

Doug is a genial, graying mining engineer who surrounds himself with maps that delineate the claims around Idaho Springs. "Clear Creek County alone has more than 1,200 gold, silver, lead, zinc, and copper mines," he said. "There are about twenty small mines working in the county now, and three mills are being remodeled and a new one built. Until they're finished, the low-grade ore will be stockpiled and the high-grade ore sent to Helena or El Paso for processing." He agreed with Bill Russell that it took a lot of "dead work" to put an old mine back into production. "It can take two years and swallow up two million dollars before any ore sees the light of day." He suggested I visit the Mendota, one of the mines he was opening, and telephoned mine superintendent Choppo Fetterhoff.

Choppo met us at the mine. We glissaded in under the raw new timbered portal on water frozen into a perfect, smooth surface between the toy-size railroad tracks, and Choppo unlocked the steel doors. Inside, it was cool, dark, gray—and very large. There were signs of new construction everywhere. We sat on benches ahead of a low electric locomotive, and Choppo piloted us into the mine.

We got off the train at a shop area and walked. "There are about a thousand feet of workings over our heads," Choppo said. "All the way to the top of the mountain. And it's been worked down to about 350 feet below us." The mountain had been hollowed, a few feet at a time, into a labyrinth. I could visualize it as a vast, three-dimensional maze, the miners zigzagging in pursuit of narrow veins of ore.

"Right back here is where that vein crosses," Choppo said. He pointed out a clear line where the gray granite gave way to darker colors and different textures. "You seldom see the silver. It's locked up with the galena, the sphalerite, the pyrite. You won't see gold in here, either." He hammered loose several chunks and handed them over. They were heavy, with crystalline facets that gleamed under our headlamps. The colors were black and silver with traces of rust and what looked like gold—but wasn't. The chunk crumbled in our hands. "That's mostly sphalerite," Choppo said, "but it would be worth processing for what gold and silver it contains."

Miners aren't the only ones who make their living near the Continental Divide. Along the way we met ranchers, alpine archaeologists, and, directly on the Divide, ski patrolmen. The price of gold notwithstanding, many of Colorado's historic mining towns —Aspen, Breckenridge, Crested Butte—have evolved into ski resorts, and the big boom is in winter recreation. Some weekends it seems that most of America's 14 million skiers are packed into cars, westbound on Interstate 70, eager to try Colorado's vast facilities for downhill skiing, cross-country skiing—even ski jumping.

I had forgotten how much fun downhill skiing can be. Breckenridge, one of the resorts closest to the Divide, is a perfect place for rediscovery: a 2,000-foot vertical drop, rapid chair lifts, packed or powder snow, and no ice or bare spots. There were miles of clean snow and groomed slopes under a clear bowl of blue sky, and when the sun was out, the air was surprisingly warm.

"When we go cross-country skiing, it's like taking a walk in the woods," Al Whately explained. I believe he was apologizing for his low-key approach, but he summed up its attraction. Our host at his ranch outside Breckenridge, Al invited me along on his daily cross-country "stroll." We enjoyed a tranquil afternoon hissing among the pines on a narrow trail that Al and his Dutch-born wife, Anneke, use nearly every day. We herringboned up onto a plateau with a clearing that commanded a view of the Divide to the east and the Tenmile Range to the west. Al described the spot as their "picnic ground." His trail joined a long cross-country trail that led from Breckenridge to Frisco, some ten miles away. We didn't go that far, as I was having trouble making turns. Every time I made the turning motions I'd learned for downhill skiing, I fell. And every time I fell, I could barely flounder to my feet; the snow was so soft there was nothing to push against. Lessons were in order.

How to fall, how to get up, how to get going—at the Breckenridge Nordic Center, instructor Charlie McCormick covered the basics. He led our class out onto the sparkling snow in a thick pine grove and proved that cross-country skiing is simple—little more than "exaggerated walking," as he said. Some simple pointers were the most helpful: control is a matter of "weighting" the area directly beneath the boot; proper adjustment of the wrist strap makes possible an efficient arm thrust; a balanced sequence of kicking and gliding makes the best use of one's energy. By the end of Charlie's lesson, all of us were gliding along concentrating not on gear and procedures but on the delights of mobility in a bright winterscape.

We went on then to try cross-country skiing at other resorts along the Divide. At Devil's Thumb, a sprawling sport ranch just below the Divide, Dick Taylor, then its enthusiastic director of skiing, told us of his dream: a system of huts similar to those in the Adirondacks and the Berkshires that would make it possible for cross-country skiers to spend days and nights in a high winter wilderness.

Sooner or later it occurs to everyone on cross-country skis that it would be fun to prolong the experience by camping in that muffled, brilliantly draped forest. Imagine watching a sunset through those trees. Imagine the stars, and the snow in the first morning light.

I well remember my first winter-camping experience: a miserable night on an Adirondack mountain, years ago, when we were so ill-informed and ill-equipped that we saw the light of morning only because we had been awake all night feeding a fire. Before I did any more camping in winter, I meant to learn more about it.

A chance to do so, under optimum conditions, soon arose. Two experienced and renowned mountaineers, Bob Craig of Keystone and Jeff Lowe of Boulder, planned a weekend of winter-survival training atop nearby Loveland Pass, at about 12,000 feet. The session was to be held for members of the Keystone and Arapahoe Basin ski schools and patrols, and Paul and I were invited along. As it happened, we would be camping exactly on the Divide. In midwinter.

Weather conditions at 8,500 feet, I had learned, have little in common with weather conditions at 12,000 feet. I drove east from Breckenridge on a bright, mild morning, thinking, as I switchbacked upward toward Loveland Pass, that we might be treated to one of those achingly clear blue-sky (Continued on page 82)

FOLLOWING PAGES: *Ice ax in hand, Mike gropes toward the head of Dexter Creek in the Uncompahgre National Forest. Even in April cascades remain frozen on the canyon's shadowed walls.*

73

In a deliberate but tricky maneuver, kayak and kayaker somersault out of End-Over-End Hole on the Arkansas River. A capsized kayaker (left) "sets up" for an Eskimo roll that will right him and his overturned craft.

FOLLOWING PAGES: Autumn bathes a slope of the Hunter-Fryingpan Wilderness with random tints. Quaking aspens, so-named for the tendency of their leaves to quiver in the slightest breeze, here turn to gold in late September.

Gourmet fixings form a sunlit still
life (right) and a portable feast for
wranglers from the Red Mountain
Horse Center and their friends
from Aspen. Here they lunch on
fruit, cheese, bread, and sautéed
chicken breasts.

*S*low and easy pace, spectacular autumn colors, and warm mountain sunshine lure riders to the Hunter-Fryingpan Wilderness. At left, they cross Van Horn Meadow during a four-day, hundred-mile pack trip that took them through forests of pine and aspen and across alpine meadows. At day's end, a rider sips coffee by the potbellied stove in the dining tent (below) as sparks swirl from its chimney.

weekends when every distant detail of the peaks stands etched in the high-elevation light. Or we might weather a stormy ordeal.

At about 10,000 feet the clouds gathered and thickened, and the first flakes began to fall. At 11,000 feet I switched on the headlights and slowed to a crawl, creeping around the curves in a near blizzard. Only when the invisible highway leveled off did I realize I had arrived at Loveland Pass. Paul and I were to meet in the small parking lot at the summit and ski to the campsite nearby. Lights of other isolated vehicles emerged from the scouring snow and passed. I guessed at the entrance to the parking lot and bucked my van over the drifts as far as I could. I found Paul's car with its wheels already drifted over. When I opened my van door to place skis and poles and pack outside, the snow flew in, drifting across the floor and seats. A perfect weekend for learning about winter survival.

Leaning into the northwest gale, I waited at the edge of the highway while a gasoline tank truck with all its lights ablaze inched and skidded past. Seeing the driver, and remembering the miles of slick, blind switchbacks below, I knew I was looking at a very brave man. When I turned to seek our campsite, I doubted I would ever find it: I couldn't see three yards. It would be at least ironic, I thought, if I got lost while searching for a winter-survival class near a federal highway. But Paul abruptly emerged from the blizzard. We traded muffled greetings, then groped our way to the campsite.

Shelter was of first importance. Paul and I arrived in time to help complete four snow caves that were being burrowed into a drifted bank. Under the guidance of Bob and Jeff, we dug straight in, keeping the entrance as small as possible. Then, leaving a two-foot-deep pit at the entrance, we dug upward to hollow out a dome. We made the floor higher than the entrance and the pit, which would allow the colder air to sink below the shelf where we would be staying.

Inside, the logic of the design was obvious. The narrow entrance kept out the wind and the blowing snow. Body heat, plus the insulating qualities of the snow itself, raised the temperature to just above freezing. The pit also provided room for dangling legs. We punched some ventilation holes above the entrance and scooped out alcoves for candles and a stove, then spread sleeping bags on the shelf.

It grew warm enough to melt the ice off boots and beards, far more comfortable than a tent in similar conditions. We pulled off our hoods and goggles and got acquainted. Jeff, a slight, 29-year-old blond, manned the stove. He is one of a family of world-class mountaineers and outdoor-equipment manufacturers, and seemed too lighthearted to have participated in Himalayan expeditions. Christopher Robinson, from California and Australia, bore a striking resemblance to actor Burt Reynolds and was second-in-command of the Keystone ski patrol. Jim Mitchell, a taciturn ski instructor and world traveler, came from near Lake Placid, New York.

Jeff scraped snow off the walls and put it in a pot on the stove. When the water boiled, he added oriental noodles, then spices, cheese, and cans of tuna. It seethed together, and when the cheese had melted, Jeff ladled it into our mugs and bowls. During dinner our candles kept flickering out, and the air seemed less than fresh. I voiced some concern about the old canary-in-the-coal-mine effect, but no one else was worried. Apparently there is a balance to be struck in snow caves between letting in sufficient oxygen and not too much cold air. But when the stove went out, we punched two more air holes.

Making arrangements for sleeping was like fitting together pieces of a puzzle. Lowe, Robinson, and I stretched out head-to-foot like parallel logs, while Mitchell occupied the curved space just above the pit. When I awakened in the morning, I took note of the fact that when Jeff woke up, he was able to start the stove and boil water for coffee without moving from his warm sleeping bag. That's planning.

When Bob and Jeff returned to their ski areas, we went along to watch them at work. Aside from dealing with accidents on the slopes, their major duty is avalanche patrol. It is impossible to spend any time in the Colorado winter without seeing how seriously the danger of avalanches is taken. There is a centralized, computerized avalanche-information center operated by the forest service, and the highway department uses 75-millimeter howitzers to destroy potential buildups before they can turn into killers, thundering down to sweep traffic off the highways.

Riding the chair lift at Arapahoe Basin with ski patrolman Harvey DeWitt, I learned that this was the third-worst year for avalanches in the West since records were begun in the 1950s. The head of the Arapahoe ski patrol, Jim Gentling, had been caught in a slide only the week before. "He rode submerged part way down one of the outside chutes," Harvey said, "and was lucky to suffer only cuts and a black eye." At the top we followed the patrol members as they "ski-controlled" in the deep, wind-driven powder. They check the cornice-like buildups of snow and then cut across them on skis "to see if anything will dislodge." To me it looked like a form of Russian roulette, and Harvey cheerfully admitted it. "We're guinea pigs," he said.

Volume, moisture content, sequence and timing of snowfalls, wind, and other factors contribute to avalanche potential. "I went to an avalanche school," Harvey told me, "but you can't learn it from books. You've got to be out on the snow every day. You've got to see how it changes, how it feels. After a while you can generally look at a buildup and see that it's loaded—that it's ready to go."

Harvey cut and started several small slides, somehow managing not to go down with them. When the snow stopped moving, we followed in his tracks down the chutes. We were above timberline, skiing steeper slants and deeper snow than I had ever seen. It was, like many acts at high elevation, both exhausting and exhilarating.

Later in the winter Paul and I stopped by several ranches in northern Colorado to see how they coped with the snow. These high-elevation ranches seemed not merely seasons but also worlds away from the dry heat of the Culberson Ranch in New Mexico. Here the cattle endure a harsh winter, sustained by baled hay that is distributed to different parts of the feeding ground each day. As often as not the feed is carried by a horse-drawn sled that seems anachronistic but makes several kinds of sense in the Colorado winter. The horses can move over most kinds of snow, and rancher Bill Ogburn told me, "In the blowing snow, when you can't see a thing, you can just give the horses their head and sit back. They'll find the feeding ground, and then find their way home."

Every morning, from the middle of November to the middle of May, Bill Ogburn and his wife, June, rise at 5 o'clock. From the kitchen window of their Parkview Mountain Ranch, they look up toward the Continental Divide. They fix breakfast, cut stovewood, and dress "for the windchill": jeans and a wool shirt, an insulated sweat shirt with hood, an insulated overall-jumpsuit, a wool hat and a scarf, insulated waterproof boots, and leather mittens with wool liners. Bill goes out to water and feed his workhorses and hitch them to a wooden sled that is as big as a room. He loads it with hay, and with June at the reins he kicks some fifty to sixty bales off the sled to feed his cattle. It takes hours, and regardless of what the weather is doing or how he feels, "You can't skip a day."

I liked the sound and slight hyperbole of the range the Ogburns see from their window—the Never Summer Mountains. It is a cluster of peaks on the Continental Divide—virtually roadless—that defines the northwestern boundary of Rocky Mountain National Park. In actual summer, the name notwithstanding, we hiked there just over the horizon from the Ogburn's ranch.

From a trail head just below 11,605-foot Red Mountain, a long trail points north, parallel to both the Never Summer ridgeline and the Colorado River. It leads to a ghost town named Lulu City, which lies in a five-mile-wide bowl. You can stand in Lulu City and look to the Divide on three sides.

On our way into Lulu City we stopped for a snack of cheese, nuts, and apples, and stayed to watch as an entire colony of gray-muzzled, yellow-bellied marmots came out to feed in a small meadow. One fat specimen after another made its way down a nearby bank. They fanned out, munching on the grass. *Marmota flaviventris* is a comic mover. These appeared overweight in their ripping fore-and-aft gallop, as if wearing heavy coats too large and loose for their frames. Occasionally one would rear up to sniff and listen.

While we watched, another actor appeared. A ground squirrel twitched down off a low bank of rocks and roots, sniffing and nipping at the grasses. Suddenly he made a short run and leaped at the blossom of a clover-like plant that grew some eight inches off the ground. The stem was no stronger than a blade of grass and would not, of course, sustain the weight of a ground squirrel. He hit the blossom a passing bite and somersaulted on over. When we laughed aloud, the marmots froze, then went on feeding.

Shortly, the marmots were interrupted again. From somewhere we heard the yapping call of a coyote. All the marmots, galvanized, left their feeding and galloped in heavy haste to their burrows. Without a backward glance they threw themselves one after the other into the openings.

Rocky Mountain National Park is a big, busy, attractive area. Like most parks it has few roads, so the ones it has tend to be crowded with long lines of campers and vans, none able to move faster than the slowest creeper. That can be exasperating in many places, but not on

Trail Ridge Road. It is so spectacular that even while minding its grades and turns you have difficulty keeping your eyes from reaching out to the skyscraping peaks, the swooping green valleys, and the succession of horizons too complex for memory. When the road ascends above timberline at about 11,000 feet, it is one of the most dramatic in the country.

In the last hours of light, during sunset and later, traffic thins out, and it is possible to look around, to watch how the darkness does not fall but instead rises from the valleys up to the ridges. We stopped at Medicine Bow Curve and gazed north under a solid storm ceiling to the dark mountains forty miles away in Wyoming. And we looked south to a horizon of darkened points and plateaus that lay just under the sunset: Mount Ida, Sprague Mountain, Stones Peak, Knobtop Mountain, Flattop Mountain. We decided to hike that long stretch of alpine tundra.

A fellow Easterner, a graphic designer named Wendy Palitz, joined us here for a few days, and, after securing supplies in Grand Lake and our permit at the Grand Lake Entrance Station, we started a long hike from the base of the Divide's west slope. Our projected route lay up the North Inlet Trail past Cascade Falls, then up Hallett Creek and the switchbacks beneath Andrews Pass.

At the lower end of this trail, a sign proclaims, "Mountains Don't Care!" It explains the hazards that may be encountered in the high country. Many of the cautions seemed obvious—never hike alone, watch for shifts in the weather—but as we hiked the dusty trail, I found myself repeating the title phrase. It seemed a useful comment on this entire project. Of course, no part of the world, whether natural or man-made, can be said to *care*. If a mountain doesn't care, then neither does a bridge or an airplane or the four walls of my own apartment. Still, it is well to be reminded that mountains are a locus of extremes, where the world goes about its business of building up and tearing down, of gestations and deaths, in powerfully indifferent ways.

We wore shorts against the heat of a very still, dry afternoon and were grateful for the deep shade of the lodgepoles and spruce. Above Cascade Falls our route became a canyon trail, with the crashing stream on one side and steep rocks and banks on the other, with mountain harebell and a kind of daisy growing at the edges of the path.

We found the turnoff trail to Lake Solitude in evening light. It had been a long, steady climb with heavy packs, and even after we found our site, we moved slowly in getting set up. Darkness overtook us before we had finished our dinner.

Our next day's climb was some 2,000 feet of sunny switchbacks that led up onto the broad back of the Divide. At about 12,000 feet, very tired, we leveled off in a sea of green grass that surrounded islands of pale boulders. It grew cloudy (Continued on page 92)

FOLLOWING PAGES: *Raising clouds of powder, ski patrolmen swoop down the North Pole Plunge in the Arapahoe Basin Ski Area. The men locate potential avalanches and attempt to disarm them.*

risly Ridge towers above a ski patrolman at Arapahoe Basin as he breaks a trail in fresh snow. At Berthoud Pass, ski patrol director Phil Sasso (below) examines layers of snow in a test pit; the extent of bonding between the layers affects avalanche potential. A hand lens (bottom) reveals different types of ice grains, which vary in stability and cohesion. At right, Breckenridge patrolmen prepare to detonate explosives to dislodge nearby snowpack.

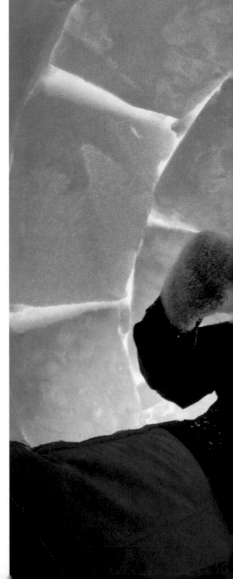

Hardened snow, blown and packed by the wind, becomes a cozy igloo for winter campers above Berthoud Pass. After setting the first layer of blocks, ski patrolman Tom Swoboda (left) levels the igloo's floor. Colleague Bob Perkins (opposite, lower) hefts a bulky slab, which he cut from the snow with the blunt, large-toothed snow saw. Little more than an hour later, Kelty Ewing and Tom add finishing touches by chinking gaps with snow.

and cool. We met other backpackers, equally tired, who had started from Bear Lake on the east side and hiked over the Divide.

Along the top the path wound north just west of the Divide, from Flattop Mountain, around Ptarmigan Point, and onto the Bighorn Flats—much of it above 12,000 feet. Toward evening the light grew cool and silvery as ominous cauliflower formations of clouds began rolling in. The path was a dry track, trod below the level of the thick green vegetation cover and worn pale and dusty. The meandering route had been marked by a succession of painstakingly built-up cairns. Arranged in pairs, they appeared in distant silhouette as haunting, primitive monuments.

The alpine tundra on top is a special, fragile ecological zone where the plant life has miniaturized in adaptation to the short season, the wind, the scant soil, and the temperature extremes that vary widely from day to night and season to season. Flowers are profuse in their small scale, and we passed clusters of tiny alpine columbine blooms, goldbloom saxifrage, and alpine forget-me-nots. Up here, living things cling as close to the ground as the skin on a peach.

We crisscrossed the flats atop the Divide for the views to either side. To the east we could see across Forest Canyon and the start of the Big Thompson River, across Trail Ridge, and out of the park to the golden farmlands on the flats east of Estes Park. To the southwest and below was the shimmering silver surface of Grand Lake. We hiked down below timberline and found a clear space for our campsite. While we ate our dinner, we watched the gathering array of storm clouds. One vast gray system seemed to be moving our way from the southwest, while a second, taller and more turbulent, appeared to rotate in place. Lines of lightning were dropping out of both systems, soundlessly touching the distant mountains, and I remembered the sign's warning about watching the weather.

In the morning we woke to a damp chill and peered out of our tents to see that a cloud had stuck on the mountain, had settled over us, a woolly gray mass of drifting moisture. We needed water for breakfast, so I took the bottles and headed toward a snowbank I'd seen the night before.

On my way back, with the bottles full, I found visibility contracting until I could barely move among the boulders without stumbling. It was as thick as the fog and clouds that had poured through the Window in the San Juans. As on that occasion, I knew there was a deep valley and a long mountain view hidden behind the gray mass. But I couldn't even locate my own camp. All the boulders that had looked like landmarks on the way out looked exactly alike on the way in. I stopped, stymied by the weather again. At last I started calling out, and after a while heard a reply. "Where are you?" Wendy shouted. "I don't know. Keep talking and I'll find you," I said. She did, and, like an airplane in a fog, I homed in on her voice.

In good hands, Buff Kidd gets a lesson from his father, Olympic silver-medalist Billy Kidd. Now Steamboat Springs' skiing director, Kidd in 1964 won the U.S. its first medal in men's competition.

3 Wyoming:

Clouds nudge a rim of the Great Divide Basin. The basin's waters divide

The Great Divide Basin

neither east nor west; precipitation here sinks into the ground.

THE FIRST TIME I slept on sand, I was at an elevation of seven thousand feet and a thousand miles from the nearest beach. Photographer Paul Chesley and I were camped on a sand dune, a long loaf of a hill patted and smoothed by the wind, which blew constantly. It created an oceanic landscape of waves and hollows—white-sand ripples of mesmerizing geometry. A sparse crop of what looked like beach grass, growing in narrow bundles of just three or four slender blades, tinted the drifts of nearby dunes. Touched by gusts of wind, each blade bent rhythmically to the surface to trace with the economy of a Japanese calligrapher a shadow arc in the sand.

We half expected, over the next dune, to see a firm blue span of ocean, but all we saw were the mountains and ridges that define the Great Divide Basin, also known as the Red Desert, of Wyoming.

When I first saw the dunes, at sunset from a campsite on Steamboat Mountain, they seemed like part of an ancient strand, a white archipelago that shimmered in the blue dusk. From my 8,000-foot-high viewpoint I could see the Killpecker Dunes—one of the largest dune areas in North America—reaching for miles east and west along the northern perimeter of the basin. During that night I noticed, out across the basin, a lightning storm flickering silently in the distance; the pinpoint lights of coal draglines and oil rigs; and a paling white reflection from that river of sand.

Later we camped on the other side of the basin, near Ferris, an abandoned petroleum camp of the 1920s. The sand was fine-grained, fit for an hourglass: dry, pure, and translucent. It is eolian, having been borne from the west by the wind. It is the legacy of a hot, dry period 5,000 to 10,000 years ago that changed the land and its life. At midday it was white and glaring hot—hard walking with the promise of hard sleeping. I had forgotten my foam sleeping pad, so when we camped I graded the humps and cones with my hands, then tried to burrow out hollows for shoulders and hips. But the sand was too loose, too fine, and it trickled back to fill the hollows.

The Great Divide Basin is a vast, dry oval in south central Wyoming. Waters do not divide here, but instead flow in and seep down. It is nearly treeless and can be very cold or very hot. The wind is often strong. It forced our attention once again to the physics of tent erection. When I raised my tent's A-frame, the open end billowed once, sharply, and jerked the metal stakes from the loose sand. The tent flattened. I used the thick, oversize stakes that had served me well in a Colorado mountain blizzard, but the wind uprooted them. I tried double stakes at a more acute angle. Again, the wind won. Paul found the solution by digging down into a subsurface level of moister, firmer sand and burying a plastic stake.

The dunes we camped on near Ferris, just a small portion of the Ferris Dune Field area, are "active" dunes. A high water table here supports a variety of vegetation that tends to stabilize the sand, but where the vegetation cover has been disturbed, or in zones where powerful winds blow, the dunes constantly shift and reform. Even these restless dunes are far from the lifeless wasteland we had expected. In the morning, after a windless night, the sand was a register of nocturnal comings and goings. We found the faint marks of hop-

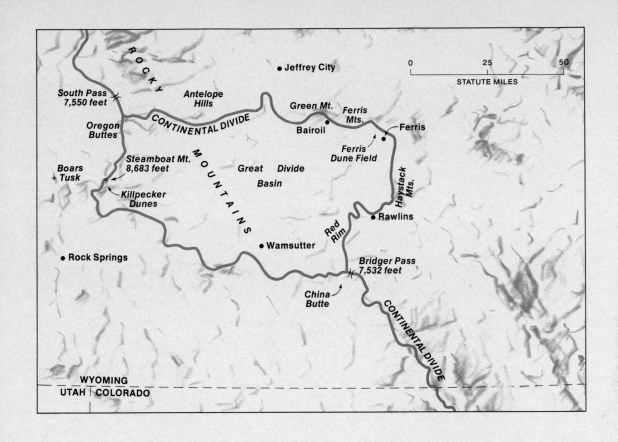

Formed by a split in the Continental Divide, the Great Divide Basin, or Red Desert, sprawls across 2,250,000 acres in south central Wyoming. The basin receives little precipitation, and its sunbaked floor hides a wealth of energy sources—coal, oil, natural gas, and uranium ore—now being developed.

ping birds, zigzagging mice, even insects. There were prints of domestic sheep, pronghorn tracks, and paw prints that were probably a coyote's. Sheep drifted among the empty houses, sage-grown walks, and derelict, bullet-punched autos in Ferris. When we left the sand to hike up and over the foothills of the nearby Ferris Mountains, herds of pronghorns came to their feet, stared, then sprinted away.

"I've walked all over the mountains, hunting elk," rancher Roy Raymond told us. "The Ferris Mountains are all straight up or straight down." His Ferris Mountain Ranch sprawls along the base of the 15-mile-long range, and his family has run cattle in the mountains for more than three decades, so he should know. Still, we thought he was exaggerating until that night: We found it difficult to locate two level places large enough for our small tents, even on the most hospitable-looking terrain at the base of the mountains where the sage hills met the pine and juniper thickets.

The next day provided a lesson in just how rugged a small mountain range can be. We explored steep-sided canyons and found ourselves performing the most exhausting bushwhacking of the

Airborne wrangler rounds up a band of wild horses on the dry flatlands of the Great Divide Basin (left). To prevent feral horses from overwhelming the basin's graze, the Bureau of Land Management captures more than a thousand here each year. People may adopt the horses, like those herded into the box canyon below, through the BLM's Adopt-A-Horse program. Above, cowboys load captured animals for the trip to a BLM holding facility in Rock Springs.

entire trip. "Hiking" isn't the word for it. Trying to stay on game trails, we pushed and ducked and slithered around one canyon wall, then up and over a high saddle into another canyon whose sides were so steep we could descend only by holding on to thick pine branches. The canyon held a freshwater spring, and we enjoyed a long, restful lunch with plenty of cool drinking water before tackling the next ascent: more scree and boot-scraping roots. Hot, hours behind our schedule, and rubber kneed from our omnidirectional scrambling, we reached the high grassy meadows and pine stands of Youngs Pass quite ready to camp for the night.

We were rewarded by our campsite, a parklike spread of lush grass sheltered by pines, with soft level ground for the tents. Nearby a cold spring rushed from the hillside to start a stream that circled our site. Broad fallen logs provided counters for cooking and benches for sitting. There were fewer mosquitoes than in the desert below. We set up camp early enough to soak our feet in the stream and to luxuriate in the long midsummer evening. The site was so unlike the sand dunes only a handful of miles away that it was difficult to believe we were still on the rim of the Great Divide Basin.

From the point at Bridger Pass south of Rawlins, where the Continental Divide splits to form the Great Divide Basin, one rim—the Pacific—stretches west, then north not far from Rock Springs. The other—the Atlantic—runs north from Rawlins into the Haystack Mountains, turns west at the Ferris Mountains, and continues westward to Green Mountain and the Antelope Hills. The two divides rejoin to enclose the basin at historic South Pass. Two-thirds of the basin is public land and the rest is private, which hikers need permission to cross. Since the basin is so dry, hikers have to carry their water supply with them. Though one could hike across the basin on straight roads or on tracks that wander to oil rigs and mines, the proposed trail route follows the Atlantic rim.

The basin holds not only all the moisture that falls upon it, but also an array of oil and natural gas wells; coal and uranium mines; old stagecoach roads; vast dry ranches, mountains, buttes, and sage flats; and a wildlife population that includes thousands of pronghorns, mule deer, coyotes, sage grouse, prairie dogs, and wild horses.

"We tried to find a route that would avoid as much new development as possible," Vernon Lovejoy said when we explored the trail route together. He is a recreation planning officer for the Rawlins District Office of the Bureau of Land Management and the man responsible for recommending trail routes around the basin. "Still, we wanted the good views from up on the rims, the easy walking, and the access to water." Though there is no way to avoid some contact with the digging and drilling and mining, Vernon—an experienced outdoorsman from West Virginia—is justly proud of his work and of the basin. After a day of scouting the sage flats, the lushly watered draws, the dunes, and the rocky rims punctuated with sheepherders' stone cairns, I had to agree with Vernon that there was no other place along the Continental Divide with the basin's variety in such a relatively confined space. We had a laugh over my expectation that it would be "just desert."

The Ferris Mountains bear a distinct mark that is visible for miles, a streaky white series of arches above the timber and below the peaks, and the proposed route of the Continental Divide Trail cuts along beneath it. "That white 'racing stripe' is Madison limestone," Robert Janssen, a geologist with the BLM, explained. "The mountains have cores of Precambrian granite that we believe may be 2.5 billion years old. They record a history of repeated inundation by ancient seas. The white limestone, for instance, was deposited on one of those sea bottoms. It was much like the kind of warm shallow marine environment found around the Bahama Islands right now. On the south flank there's also Tensleep sandstone, the Amsden formation, and some shale units." We hiked across those deposits, where layers of white and brown and red rock protruded from the earth. But the geology of the basin signifies more than an interesting hiking environment: It also means energy.

"We have coal, natural gas, oil, and uranium in and around the basin," Robert told me. "The coal and oil were formed in the standard manner of hydrocarbons, as decaying organic matter from ancient swamps or deltas. Much of the gas probably originated in a low-temperature metamorphosis of the coal. The uranium, though, is different. It's an element and probably has its origin in volcanic ash. Formations containing uranium in the basin were deposited around the same time that major volcanic events were occurring in the Absaroka Range near Yellowstone. Uranium from this ash is thought to have been reworked and concentrated by groundwater."

Dave Oliver, the senior geologist for Western Nuclear, elaborated as he drove me down into the McIntosh Pit, a surface mine on the north rim of the basin south of Jeffrey City. "Uranium is a metal, a very common element, and granite is a good source of it. That means the Rocky Mountains have a high level of background radiation. But uranium that is concentrated enough to mine—that is not common. It was consolidated by groundwater movement. What we're mining here is, on the average, 0.11 percent concentrated ore."

"All mining is dangerous," Dave had reminded me at the top of the pit, as he handed me a hard hat and rubber boots with steel toes. He also showed me how to use a "self-rescuer," an optimistically named device that, in an emergency, would enable me to breathe in the presence of carbon monoxide.

We walked down an inclined shaft. Lighted only by our battery-powered headlamps, it was a twilight catacomb, gray, muddy, and dusty at once. The heavy black metallic ore is found in thin "lenses," or veins, along with quartzite, hematite, and feldspar. Arrows spray-painted by geologists pointed out the ore for the miners. A cobweb of steel mesh was pinned to the ceiling to keep slabs of rock from crashing down.

The ventilation fans were deafening, louder and harsher than an express subway at close range. With nowhere to go and nothing to absorb it, the sound beat through the shafts. The fans are essential, however, to remove the radon gas that is emitted within the mine. The ventilation pipes whistling and (Continued on page 107)

Bleating and squirming, a pronghorn fawn struggles with wildlife researchers. After capturing the pronghorns (top), researchers will affix ear tags and collars to them to help in mapping their territory. An adult (above) bolts for freedom, blood from a recently shed horn sheath staining the snow: the animals lose the sheaths naturally each winter. By learning more about the pronghorns' range and habitat, the study team hopes to determine what impact proposed coal mining in the basin will have on them.

Wind-furrowed sands of the Ferris Dune Field undulate in ever changing patterns near the basin's eastern rim (right). Wisps of Indian rice grass, whose roots may reach down several feet to fine-grained sand, help to anchor the rippled surface. Winds here have attained some of the highest speeds ever recorded in the continental United States. Mike and Colorado hiker Susan Johnson (above) brace themselves against gusts as they cross the dunes.

roaring here and there on the flanks of Green Mountain are exhausting the gas. In concentration it is carcinogenic, and in the past it has been a hazard to miners. As it emerges into the daylight, mining engineers say, it is no more dangerous than the background radiation of the Rocky Mountains.

The ore itself is trucked to a mill near Jeffrey City, where it is refined to yellowcake, a powder more than 99 percent pure that is used to make U-235 pellets, which fuel nuclear power plants.

Booms and rig rats are nothing new in the Great Divide Basin. Men first drilled for oil here in the 1880s, and the 1920s were black-gold bonanza years that spawned oil camps such as Ferris, where we had camped, and Bairoil, where I watched crews working on new oil wells. In those early days the oil and gas were extracted from comparatively shallow levels, 5,000 to 6,000 feet. Currently, drillers are reaching down through older deposits to bring up gas and oil from as deep as 20,000 feet. Finding accumulations at that level is a blend of geological mapping, seismic surveying, and luck.

Once oil is found, the drilling stops and a complex and expensive process of pumping begins. I watched one morning as a crew removed the last 10,000 feet of steel drill pipe from a bright blue rig just outside Bairoil. It was pulled up by a derrick in thirty-foot sections seven inches in diameter. Each weighed about two tons and was very slippery with mud and water and crude oil. Stripped to the waist in the sun, the five-man crew hosed off each section. Then, using chains and toothed clamps, they unthreaded it from the section below, rigged it to the derrick, and skidded it onto a shoulder-high platform. Their moves were as sure and repetitious as a rehearsed dance, even on the slippery platform, and they took only a few minutes to add another section to the stack.

Many of the cold blue lights that I had seen from my campsite on Steamboat Mountain belonged to a coal mine operated by the Northern Energy Resources Company (NERCO) and by the Jim Bridger power plant just outside the basin. The act of naming a 2,500-megawatt coal-fired, steam-driven electric generating station for the man I've always considered the craftiest, most atavistic, most unregenerate of all the wild-and-woolly mountain men, seemed to me an act close to travesty, and that made it irresistible: I had to visit this power plant.

Pure air remains one of the glories of the West. As an eastern urbanite I was unaccustomed to breathing anything I couldn't see, but I had found that the crystalline air along the Divide was a stimulant, a tonic, a builder of disconcerting appetites, and I worried that its clarity was being compromised by the effluent from smelters, forest fires, volcanoes, automobile exhausts, and power plants.

"We located the plant here because this is where the coal is," plant manager Don Vincent told me. "Also, we at Pacific Power and Light

Weathered fragments of sedimentary rock tilt toward the basin. Geologists date the formation of the ridge to a time some 65 million years ago. Rust-colored lichens speckle the jagged slabs.

107

see no point in locating a power plant in a city. We build in rural areas and transmit the power to the cities." The plant's four stacks are equipped with precipitators that remove more than 99 percent of the fly ash from the plumes, but three of the four are still uncontrolled for the emission of sulfur dioxide. To comply with standards of the Wyoming Department of Environmental Quality, the plant must remove at least 75 percent of the sulfur dioxide in those three stacks by the late 1980s.

The opacity of the smoke plume is another factor regulated by state standards. "The allowable opacity of a plume is 20 percent," Chuck Collins, engineering supervisor for air quality at the department, told me. "At times, the emissions from the Jim Bridger stacks reach that degree of opacity, and, under certain meteorological conditions, the plume doesn't disperse. It can be seen for some distance downwind of the plant.

"But the plant itself, as such plants go, is a clean one."

I rode into the open pits of the NERCO mine with engineer Steve Beil. Three massive draglines, with the lights I had seen in the night from 15 miles away, work around the clock. They strip off the overburden—all of the sandstone and shale from the surface down to the coal seam, which in this case is about 120 feet deep.

"We store the topsoil," Steve said. "We're required by law to return the land to its pre-mining condition. We don't have to get the exact original contours. We can't put this hill back *exactly* as it was. But we are required to recontour and revegetate the land." He showed me where the new hills and swales had been graded and seeded with shrubs and wheatgrass. Irrigation pipes were in place.

"You can't get the coal out and still keep the other resources," BLM area manager Ed Coy said, explaining the difficulty of mining coal and at the same time protecting the wildlife and other natural resources. The BLM is squarely astride the conflicts that are developing among the energy interests, the ranchers, and the environmentalists over the uses of public land and the resources thereon—and under. As manager of the Overland Resource Area, Ed walks the line among conflicting needs and conflicting responsibilities: The BLM has charge of range management, mineral rights, recreation, wildlife, and other resources on public lands. The balancing act is rendered doubly difficult by the checkerboard pattern of land ownership in the southern half of the basin. Each square mile of public land is adjacent to a square mile of private land. The checkerboard is a legacy of a 19th-century act that granted federal land to the railroads as encouragement and financial incentive to build transcontinental rail lines. It is a legacy that all but confounds development of land-use policies.

Ed Coy had just come from a meeting where the impact of coal mining in the Red Rim–China Butte area had been discussed. "There are seven ranchers involved. Coal mining would *affect* their ranches, but it wouldn't put any of them out of business; they would be compensated for the inconvenience. Mining would require agreement between the surface owner and the owner of the mineral rights."

Portions of the Red Rim–China Butte area are thought to be

critical winter range for the basin's large population of pronghorns. Several state and federal agencies and a power company are supporting the University of Wyoming in a study of pronghorn ecology in the area, in an effort to determine how coal mining will affect the animals. A helicopter is used to herd them into traps, where researchers equip some with radio collars and others with neckbands, to facilitate tracking. A veterinarian takes a blood sample from some of the animals to look for diseases. About 2,400 pronghorns winter in the Red Rim–China Butte area and, like the ranchers, their lives are bound to be affected by an increase in coal mining.

Four-footed creatures of another sort—mustangs—also roam the basin. "They're not really 'mustangs' as such; the Spanish-blood horses are long gone," John Winter told me. We were at the BLM Rock Springs corral for wild horses, and John is the BLM's wild horse specialist. "They're feral horses, mostly ranchers' stock that over the years have wandered off."

"Then are they really wild?" I asked.

"Yer darn tootin' they are. They go completely wild in a year or less, and the ranchers have an awful time catchin' 'em." We were watching some of John's cowboys cut a young, well-muscled gray stallion out of a small herd. "They'll kick, bite, run over you, run under you...." The gray stallion broke into a run and friskily outpaced the men. "Yeah," John observed. "It gets pretty western out here sometimes."

There are probably 10,000 feral horses in Wyoming, several thousand in the Great Divide Basin alone, and the number is growing. Ranchers want them off the checkerboard rangeland, and the BLM and wildlife observers worry that the prolific horses will exhaust the graze. So, by local agreement, John's cowboys round up between one and two thousand a year. After worming, vaccinating, and branding them, the BLM puts the animals up for adoption on a first-come, first-served basis and charges $22 a head to cover veterinary costs.

We had seen them everywhere, always in small herds of four to eight horses, always grazing warily. There were all types and colors, but most resembled quarter horses: sturdily built and fast. I approached a group near the base of Steamboat Mountain, but they walked away, watching me carefully. All looked vigorous and strong. "They're healthy as heck," John told me. "They go through hellacious winters, right up there with the elk and the pronghorns. And they've got a good genetic pool out there; there's not a whole lot of inbreeding.

"Adoptions are limited to four horses a person, and people come from all over—Texas, Tennessee, California. We screen them. If they don't have a suitable truck, for instance, we send them home. And we follow up the adoption with questionnaires. Most work out, but sometimes we get a horse back. Maybe a neighbor reports that it's being abused or not fed or something.

"We round them up with a helicopter," John continued, "and it takes a lot of the fun out of roundup. We use the chopper to get them started and then hang back. The horses don't run too hard, and the colts can keep up and stay together. Then, about a mile from the corral, we bring them in with outriders."

Under a yellow dawn I watched a roundup among the sage-thick rims southeast of Rock Springs. Pilot Ron Shane dipped into the narrow draws to flush a herd of some two dozen horses into the open and start them toward the narrowing neck of wire fence that led to a holding corral. The brown and gray and white horses loped ahead of the helicopter noise and clustered tightly around their herd leader, a wiry gray stallion. The BLM cowboys rode in behind them and whooped and yelled, their voices rising along with their dust into the early sky. Once in the corral the horses milled around, some of them nipping and kicking at each other. They were magnificent animals, restless and full of spirit and without fear.

On my last day in the Great Divide Basin I explored the dry hills in the northwestern corner, from Steamboat Mountain to the Oregon Buttes and on to South Pass. In Pine Canyon shy wild horses stood and grazed around the scattered silver gas wells. A cave—an obvious shelter under the pale cliffs—contained petroglyphs, faint geometric carvings, as well as the latter-day graffiti of initials and dates and recent deer scat: signs that over the years people and animals had passed this way. But on this dusty afternoon the silence and the solitude were complete.

Out beyond Pine Canyon I scrambled up the Boars Tusk, a snag of volcanic rock that rises straight and dark from the plain. The rock looked spongy and was nearly black, except where it had been limed by generations of birds. I was startled to come upon the flattened, dry remains of two adult sheep: bones, teeth, and pelts that were incongruously fresh—seemingly ready for carding and weaving. Victims of the weather? Coyotes? Sickness?

I wished for more time to wander in the Oregon Buttes, the jumble of stark hills that are visible for miles along the trails that cross South Pass. Long the most important crossing of the Continental Divide, the pass is as shallow and undramatic in appearance as any other sage flat in the West. But it is a name to conjure with, and it was—and remains—a kind of continental junction. Traces of transcontinental trails are still visible on the ground, and ever since the mountain men first ventured here in 1824, thousands of people have crossed South Pass seeking land, gold, and freedom. The Mormon Trail, the Oregon Trail, the California Trail, the Pony Express, and now Route 28 traverse the same ground. There are historical markers to go with the stagecoach station sites and the crumbling log ranch buildings. South Pass is now a registered national historic landmark, a tourist stopover, tamed and mellowed by time.

Watery plume spews from a natural gas well near Wamsutter. Orin Winders, an Amoco employee, vents water vapor and ice plugs from the frozen wellhead. Pipelines carry the gas to the Midwest.

FOLLOWING PAGES: *Snow dusts gully-carved hills east of Rock Springs. A local pilot calls such country "typical western Wyoming: sparse vegetation and prairie dogs."*

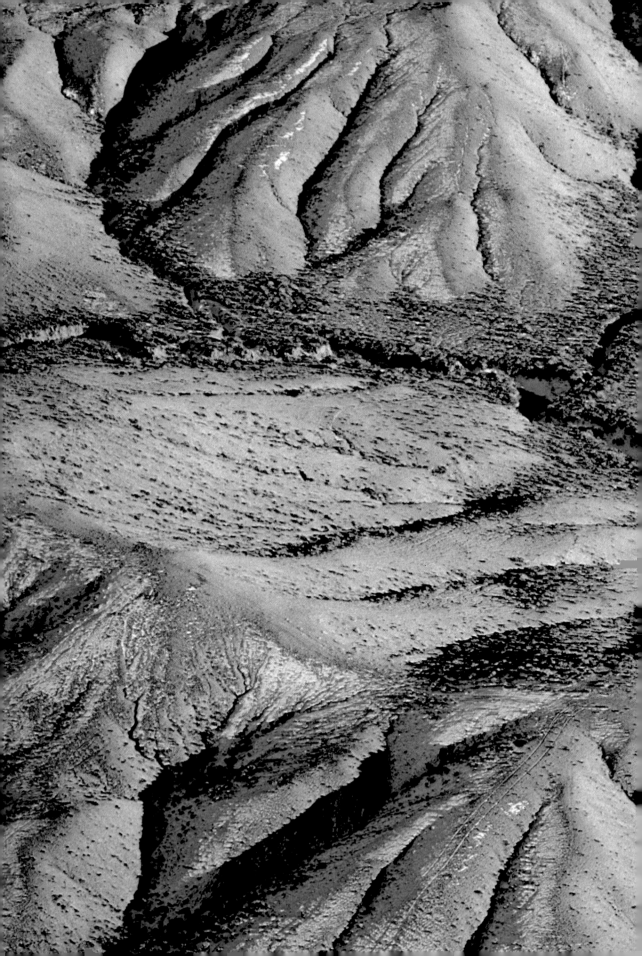

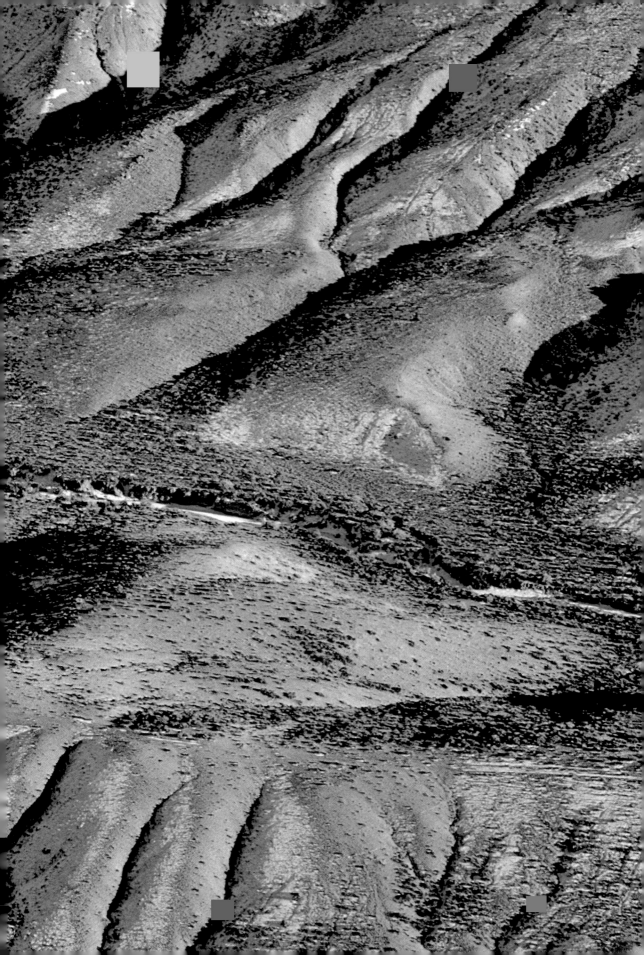

4 Wyoming: The Wind

Guide Glenn Milner inches up a face of the Wind River Range. Glenn

WHEN YOU STAND in the historic footprints of pioneers at South Pass, surrounded by sage flats, you feel no sense of being on one of the early routes to the West—until you turn north and look at the Wind River Range. In those massed, hard peaks of dry stone and year-round ice, you can see that here mountain means barrier. For more than a hundred miles northward from South Pass, the Wind River Range lies astride the Continental Divide like a jagged wall. There are more glaciers here than in any other stretch of the Rocky Mountains—in all, more than sixty.

After encircling the Great Divide Basin, the Continental Divide angles northwestward atop the peaks and glacial ridges of these mountains. It separates the Popo Agie, a Wind River tributary, from the Big Sandy, the Green, and the Snake, rivers familiar to the beaver-trapping mountain men and settlers bound for California and Oregon. It touches the highest summits in Wyoming, including Gannett Peak at 13,804 feet, and along the way looks like everyone's notion of the Great Divide: remote, alpine, inaccessible, and unforgiving.

Above the highway at Togwotee Pass, the Divide loops eastward toward the Absaroka Range, then cuts northwestward through one of the largest remote areas in the lower 48 states. In Yellowstone National Park, it angles westward over forested, jumbled plateaus left over from eons of volcanic blasts and flows, passing thermal basins, lakes, and a backcountry teeming with wildlife.

The Wind River Range—or the Winds, as they're called—are at once remote and selectively crowded. The trail heads at Big Sandy Opening and Elkhart Park are jammed during the summer months, and many people visit the Cirque of the Towers or use the Highline Trail and its offshoots, but everyone either is on foot or on horseback. They are here to hike, climb, ski, hunt, fish, or just *be* in these rugged mountains. That it takes muscle just to get into the Winds creates some community of feeling.

My 15-year-old daughter, Molly, and I sat akimbo in our tent near Seneca Lake. The day's 11-mile hike had included a 1,500-foot climb, and we were tired but not yet sleepy. We had retired to the shelter of the tent because the mountain air was cloudy with bloodthirsty mosquitoes. Rain had begun to fall, and a major thunderstorm was working its way toward us, walking north along the Winds like a huge lightning-legged creature. We had borrowed a deck of worn cards, and by the light of our lone candle, Molly — who claimed she had not played gin rummy since our last camping trip—was shutting me out. In the night outside the tent, the air was restless with ozone. We could hear the quiet murmur of voices from the other tents in our group and a background grumble of thunder.

A scream slashed the air. It started *(Continued on page 122)*

From South Pass, landmark to mountain men and wagon masters, the Continental Divide enters a haven of federal lands in Wyoming's glacier-crowded Wind River Range. It climbs the granite slopes of 13,804-foot Gannett Peak, the highest in the state, then enters the thermal wonderland of Yellowstone National Park.

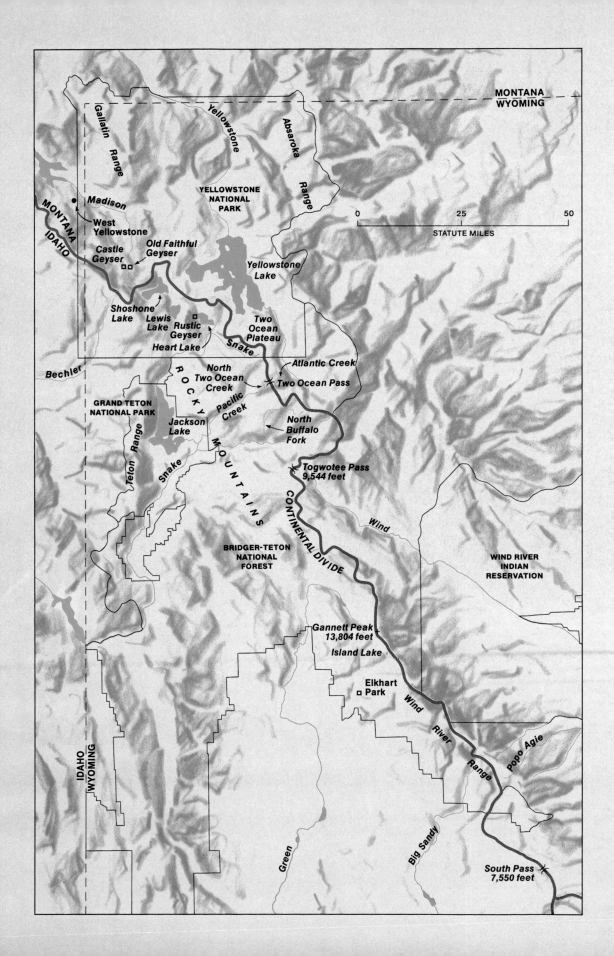

MONTANA
WYOMING

Gallatin Range

Yellowstone

Absaroka Range

YELLOWSTONE
NATIONAL
PARK

MONTANA
IDAHO

Madison

West
Yellowstone

0   25   50

STATUTE MILES

Castle
Geyser

Old Faithful
Geyser

Yellowstone
Lake

Shoshone
Lake

Lewis
Lake

Rustic
Geyser

Heart Lake

Two
Ocean
Plateau

Snake

Atlantic Creek

Bechler

North
Two Ocean
Creek

Two Ocean Pass

R O C K Y

GRAND TETON
NATIONAL PARK

Pacific
Creek

North
Buffalo
Fork

Teton Range

Jackson
Lake

Snake

M O U N T A I N S

Togwotee Pass
9,544 feet

Wind

BRIDGER-TETON
NATIONAL
FOREST

CONTINENTAL DIVIDE

WIND RIVER
INDIAN
RESERVATION

Gannett Peak
13,804 feet

Island Lake

Elkhart
Park

IDAHO
WYOMING

Wind

River

Popo Agie

Range

Green

Big Sandy

South Pass
7,550 feet

While snow melts on a warm July day, beginners learn basic climbing techniques on gentle slopes in the Titcomb basin of the Wind River Range. Mike rappels (above) under Glenn Milner's watchful eye. A blindfold (right) increases Mike's awareness of the rock's surface textures and improves his balance and the coordination of his hands and feet. Opposite, blindfolded students feel their way up a granite incline. Before his death, Glenn worked for five years as a guide and climbing instructor in the western mountains and in Alaska. Asked once why he risked the hazards of climbing, he said: "If I didn't, I'd risk not living."

At Island Lake, climbers turn to fishing for relaxation. Angling below the lake (right), Dr. William Thompson had his luck play out along with his line: The feathered barb snagged in his earlobe (below). Guy Toombes and Glenn Milner numbed the ear with snow, then carefully snipped the shaft (bottom) and removed the hook with tweezers. Bill's luck changed later in the day, when he caught these golden trout (left).

as a razor keening, high and edgy, then descended through a devilish, throaty squall. Molly and I froze, staring round-eyed in the candle-light. I felt as fluffed up as a scared cat. From another tent, a quavery question floated: "What was *that*?" We waited, listening. Then the answer occurred to everyone at once: a mountain lion.

The cry had sounded quite close, but no one was certain of the distance or direction. We waited, watching the flares of lightning, but the scream was not repeated. A little later, between rolls of thunder, a pack of coyotes began yapping somewhere above us.

In the morning I crawled out of the tent to find that the overnight rain had dampened everything except the ardor of the mosquitoes. We ate a cold breakfast and quickly struck camp; everyone was eager to outhike the insects to our destination at Titcomb basin, where we would do some climbing. We were going there with Dr. William Thompson and his Jackson Hole Mountain Guides, Guy Toombes and Glenn Milner.

High trails in the Winds traverse busy terrain. If the entire mountain chain had never been named, it surely would have been called "rocky" by the first person hiking through the cluttered basins from, say, Knife Point Mountain to Mount Sacagawea. The valleys and benches in the shadows of these 13,000-foot peaks are strewn with the detritus of glacial erosion.

The sunken trail changed direction every few feet as it rose over rims and glacial debris, scalloped around gneiss boulders, circled ponds and lakes, and bucked directly through boulder fields. Views changed with every yard among the white and gray and beige rocks; shots of light gleamed from embedded quartz and mica.

According to geologists, crustal forces working some 45 to 65 million years ago created the Wind River Range. No sooner had the mountains been uplifted than stream erosion began tearing them down. On the flanks of the mountains, basins and valleys were filled and leveled. During a recent age of geological activity, these level areas were uplifted into the high benches that are characteristic of the mountains, and along which the Highline Trail winds. The intervals of glaciation during the past million years did not touch the highest peaks, but several times the trail upon which we were hiking was buried beneath a layer of ice a thousand feet thick. Even now there are glaciers among the highest peaks along the Divide—Fremont, War-ren, Gannett, and Dinwoody—but these are latecomers that date from several hundred years ago to only the middle of the last century.

The Wind River mountains are made of reliable rock: granite, gneiss, pegmatite veins, dark quartz diorite, and migmatite, a swirled mixture of metamorphic and igneous rocks that reminded me of blended ice cream. These are less brittle than sedimentary rock, and provide trustworthy holds. The gritty texture makes the rock adhesive to the hands and feet. Therefore the Winds—with their cirques, walls, peaks, and towers—are a favorite range with serious climbers.

Despite the fact that Bill, Guy, and Glenn had been coming to Titcomb basin for 12 years and had scaled every peak many times, they were eager to reach our campsite, get set up, and start climbing.

That first evening near Island Lake, with packs shed and supper under way, Guy and Glenn raced to some nearby truck-size erratics to do a little "bouldering." They addressed the rock faces with fingertips, palms, and toes, and made quick ascents. "You just can't keep these guys from climbing rocks," Bill said. I joined them and we spent an hour trying abbreviated routes up the rocks. For me, bouldering offered the fun of climbing — solving problems by combinations of moves and holds — without the need for worrying about a misstep.

After a day in camp at Titcomb basin, Glenn Milner gathered his gear for some serious climbing instruction. His students lined up and faced a fissured slope of buff granite. Sectioned by horizontal cracks and streaked with moisture, it rose at what appeared to be a 30-degree angle. Glenn's first suggestion was that we climb the slope in our bare feet. It would give us a better feel for the rock, he said. I started up and indeed found it easier to detect and grip the cracks and facets with soft feet than with the soles of my sneakers.

"Now tie your bandannas over your eyes, and no cheating," Glenn said. "I want you to climb it blind." We didn't believe him. We objected. We wouldn't be able to see where we were going, or "read" the slope. We'd slip and fall. Glenn was obdurate.

Blindfolded, I groped onto the rock face and paused to sort out the sensations. It seemed steeper than when I'd been looking. Glenn cautioned us to stay well up on all fours and to keep our weight out. I paused until I could feel the slant and texture of the rock, the pull of gravity, the push of the wind, and the set of my body on the rock. Then I began to climb. It worked. It was a confidence-builder, and after climbing blind, going up with all my senses in use was easy.

By then we had plenty of confidence in Glenn, who was energetic, lively, funny, and looked to be strong enough to *carry* us over the Divide, if need be.

The next day, before we could start climbing, we were interrupted by a call for help. Bill, who is an avid and accomplished fly-fisherman, had gone to try his luck in a stream below the lake. But he had gotten more than his customary yardage of line and leader snapping back and forth overhead and had snagged the fly in his right earlobe. He continued fishing for a couple of hours, then hiked back to camp for help in removing it. Predictably, there were suggestions that he sever the hook and *wear* the bright fly, or even match it with another in his left ear.

That afternoon Molly and I spent a long time mountain-watching. It occurred to me that during the entire course of my Continental Divide trip, I had spent more time just watching the mountains than doing anything else. Mountains rarely change enough to be noticeable within the lifetime of one person, but the light changes their appearance moment by moment, altering colors and shadows.

We were about fifty feet short of timberline, somewhere around 11,000 feet. The last tenacious trees held scruffy foliage above the granite ledges just overhead. From where we watched, the Winds slanted up from nearby for maybe a thousand feet at about a 45-degree slope. There were fissures, juts, ledges, domes, and straight cliffs. There were layers and levels, vast fault systems, and talus slopes filed

Rain-drenched riders ford North Two Ocean Creek in the Bridger-Teton National

Forest. The left branch runs eventually to the Pacific Ocean, the other to the Atlantic.

to conical points. At around 12,000 feet the angle of ascent on most peaks steepened to about 75 degrees, and the gray-tinted brown rock gathered into a distinctly vertical grain as it rose and sharpened into lean spires, peaking in faceted points that looked as edged and sharp as freshly chipped arrowheads. On invisible ledges, bright dots of snow lay clean against the warm brown rock.

I am often surprised at the colors on the mountains. Black and white seem more appropriate for such unyielding masses. But hours later, when the light on the peaks has changed, the colors and shapes are so altered that we might be looking at a new range.

Dick Olmstead, another guide in our group, was dressed like an Andean shepherd. He was free-climbing a twenty-foot wall, flowing up with the assured moves of a spider. Two student climbers tried the same route. Both got balked part way up and had to peel away from the face, dangling on the belay rope. Dick rated the climb about 5.8 (on a difficulty scale of 6), but described a sequence of moves and holds he believed would work. Challenged, I decided to try it.

Tied to the rope, I stepped onto the rock ledge. I reached into a vertical crack with my right hand and edged upward on good foot-holds. I did fine until I tried to straighten up from a crouch to reach overhead for a handhold that Dick said was there but that I couldn't see. I groped for it but didn't connect. My right arm began shaking. I couldn't hold against the rock. I peeled off, to bounce on the belay rope. I tried again later, but a pulled muscle in my back foiled me and halted my attempts at climbing for a while.

When our three-day stay in Titcomb basin had come to an end, Molly and I chanced to be the first to pack up, and, since we expected to hike out slowly, we left before anyone else. We knew the others would overtake us.

Again we passed through zones of fierce mosquito attacks, this time with repellent running low. Curious, I tallied the damage. On my right arm alone, from wrist to shoulder: 53 bites. I decided not to count anymore.

Characteristically, Glenn Milner was the first to overtake Molly and me. He came pumping along in shorts and a white sun visor and slowed to hike with us. We talked about climbing and about meeting in New York to hear some jazz. Then he went on, and we watched him churn away, each brisk step raising a puff of dust.

I still see Glenn that way, but we never got together again. Only four weeks after our climbing trip, Glenn was swept to his death by a rockfall near a summit in the Tetons.

Trail riding doesn't require much horsemanship, even when you are packing 27 miles into the Bridger-Teton National Forest. You need only alertness, endurance, and toughness—in certain areas. Paul and I were eager to see the spot below Yellowstone National Park where North Two Ocean Creek divides into Atlantic Creek and Pacific Creek—the one place along the Continental Divide where flowing water can be seen actually dividing.

We started before daylight with affable, capable wrangler Sam Ward leading two packhorses. Behind them, Paul was riding Nugget,

Rough-hewn sign, bolted to a spruce at the fork of North Two Ocean Creek, marks the point where the Continental Divide manifestly lives up to its name: Here the continent's waters visibly part.

and I was aboard TV, a 16-year-old gelding. TV stayed just off the pace and dropped back steadily until I nudged him hard enough to induce a bone-shaking trot.

We were entering a vast roadless area along the Divide that is used seasonally by fishermen and hunters, but by few others. The trail is a long, gradual climb, all of it below timberline. It follows North Buffalo Fork and then Pacific Creek through valleys, under hillsides thick with lodgepoles, and across broad meadows where willows grow. Rain dropped steadily from ragged clouds that roofed the valleys and snagged on treetops and ridges. In places the depressed trail was twenty feet wide, and, where the rain had not made it a brimming trough, it had been turned to deep mud by the horses. I understood the antipathy that exists between horse-packers and backpackers; for hikers, the trail would have been a nightmare.

While we were looking for a place to have lunch, we heard a peculiar rippling explosion from the pine-covered hills on our right. Sam said it was a tree falling: "Finally gave up standin' there." We rode on, and I remembered the old puzzle about a tree falling in the forest and the sound it doesn't make. When we halted in a grove of young pines, Sam found enough dry wood for a fire, and I discovered that the rain had entered my boots, poncho, and saddlebags. At lunch, Sam's fire dried our fronts while the rain wet our backs.

The afternoon weather included three hail showers, and out in the meadows the rain beat straight down. There was nothing to do but ride along under it and thank your hat. During the two hours it took to ride the length of North Fork Meadows, Sam—who was reared on a ranch in Colorado—asked me how I liked this country. I told him I thought it was beautiful. "Isn't it? I love it," he said. "If I'd been born a hundred years ago, I'd have spotted me a nice cabin up here in the trees, and I'd have had the whole valley."

Sam's indomitable spirit was as welcome as his multiple skills. At the end of the afternoon the rain let up just as we stopped for the day. Sam split a lodgepole and got a fire going for heat, morale, and coffee. I staggered a bit while erecting our tent; that day was the longest I had ever spent on a horse, and since early afternoon my legs had felt spiraled too far the wrong way.

Around the fire we arranged boots, socks, gloves, rain pants, hats, and ponchos for drying. Then we settled to a supper of elk steaks, beef steaks, fried onions and "taters," fresh brownies, and boiled coffee. After that, neither the coffee nor the fact that we were in prime grizzly country could keep us awake past nine.

The rain resumed at dawn. After breakfast we rode farther up through the lodgepole forest. In pale light and drifting fog, the wet pine needles appeared to drip silver into silver pools and onto the soaking forest floor. Just below a shallow ford, the rushing cold stream of North Two Ocean Creek met a rooted point and divided into Atlantic Creek and Pacific Creek. Left and right, the waters really did part. It was an idea at last made real. Bolted to a tree was a sign that read: "Parting of the Waters. Atlantic Ocean 3488. Pacific Ocean 1353." The mileages referred to the distances the waters had to travel, following their zigzag courses, to reach their respective oceans.

These streams are tributaries of two rivers, the Yellowstone and the Snake, at the heart of the old mountain fur-trade territory. This may not be the most remote place on the Continental Divide, but on that early morning, with the rain hissing in the pines, it felt like it.

At the north end of the Wind River Range, the Continental Divide descends to the high forested plateaus of Yellowstone National Park. Nowhere in its westward crossing of the park does it surmount the lodgepole timberline. It remains in remote wildlife areas, skirts several fine lakes, and passes near two of the three major active backcountry thermal basins. The trail goes directly through these bizarre zones of boiling springs, steaming creeks and mud pots, rearing geysers, and hellish odors.

John Colter, who crossed the continent with the Lewis and Clark Expedition, was the first to describe the fires and smokes and smells of the Yellowstone country. Though it's hard to tell from his account exactly where he was, Colter was probably among the first white men to see the Wind River Range, until that time the exclusive territory of Indians. The Shoshone lived in the Green River basin southwest of the Winds, and across the Divide were the Absaroka, or Crow. Indians and whites met when fur trappers began probing into the mountains in the early 1800s, (Continued on page 138)

Frothing Two Ocean Falls cascades 35 feet in Bridger-Teton, sculpting a glade garnished by scarlet Indian paintbrush. Horse-packers pause for lunch at the brink of the waterfall.

Mike emerges from early morning haze at pine-ringed Heart Lake in Yellowstone National Park. In 1980 some two million people visited Yellowstone, the oldest national park in the United States. About seventy miles of Continental Divide Trail winds through the park. More than half the world's known geysers and hundreds of fumaroles, hot springs, and other thermal features lie within Yellowstone's 3,472 square miles.

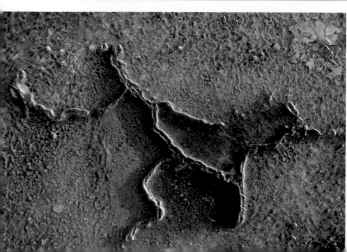

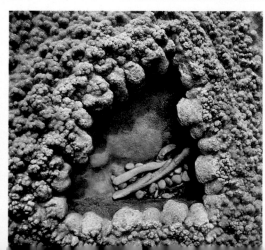

On the edge of Columbia Spring, ranger Tim Stone cautions Mike: Thin crusts may give way to boiling water, and fragile features shatter beneath heavy treads. Geyserite, deposits from thermal springs (left), forms in bizarre shapes and colors.

FOLLOWING PAGES: Like a thin snake, the Bechler River crawls through the southwestern corner of Yellowstone Park. Sandhill cranes nest here in Bechler Meadows, and cutthroat trout lure fly-fishermen to nearby fast-flowing streams.

ooling off and fleeing from insects, elk refresh themselves in the Madison River as park visitors enjoy a close look. Their bath finished, calves depart with their mother (right). Some 20,000 elk live in the park in summer. In winter about half move to feeding grounds at lower elevations outside the boundaries.

and some of them also joined the trappers at their annual gathering, the rendezvous, a boisterous reunion held each summer until 1840. Rendezvous is a thing of the past now, and so is the life led by the Indians and the mountain men. But Yellowstone remains.

At Heart Lake Geyser Basin, not far from Two Ocean Plateau in the wild southeastern corner of the park, Paul and I cautiously approached Columbia Spring with seasonal ranger Tim Stone. Like many hot pools, this one was rimmed with fragile, overhanging mineral deposits. A breakthrough into the steaming water could be fatal, and the backcountry thermal areas—unlike the heavily visited formations at Old Faithful and along the Firehole River—are not protected by boardwalks and guardrails.

"The colors tell the temperature," Tim said. "A pale aquamarine like this means it's one of the really hot ones. Darker, brighter colors, the browns and yellows, are from algae that grow in comparatively cooler pools." Three furry black bodies were rotating slowly, deep in the currents of the brimming pool. It was difficult to identify them through the shimmering water. "They're voles, I think," said Tim. "One of the larger species."

"Animals do fall in these pools once in a while," he continued. We saw large white bones on the bottom—"Elk bones," said Tim— even parts of antlers.

A sulfurous smell accompanied the vapors drifting from Columbia Spring, from Rustic Geyser, and from the other thermal openings along the northwestern shore of Heart Lake. I asked about the sources of the odors, the water, and the heat.

"They come from thousands of feet down," Tim said. "What you see is groundwater that drained downward until it approached magma, or molten rock. Then it became superheated and was pressured back up through this network as steam or hot water. It brings minerals with it." Tim indicated the gravelly deposits around the pool: "This is mostly silica, or geyserite. You can smell the sulfur."

The minerals settle in coral-like shapes along the walls of the pools and line the streams that drain the thermal areas. Everything that touches the water—pebbles, sedges, bones—is soon coated with silica and other minerals.

"There is talk now of drilling just outside the park boundaries to develop geothermal sources of energy," Tim mentioned. "But some of us are concerned that the drilling would tap into the sources of the geysers—they are very complicated—and affect the whole system by letting the pressure out."

Old Faithful suggests a timeless stability, but we found Yellowstone to be a place of instability and change. The famous geyser discharges not exactly on the hour but at intervals of anywhere from 40 to 140 minutes. Most of the 300 other geysers in the park also "play" at irregular intervals. There are more than 10,000 thermal features here — hot springs, mud pots, and fumaroles — most of which are slowly changing. Every year several thousand earth tremors are recorded in the park, most of them too small to be of consequence.

But major earthquakes as recently as 1959 and 1975 changed landforms, waterflow patterns, and active and inactive geysers. It has been 70,000 years since there was a volcanic eruption in Yellowstone, geologists say, but Mount St. Helens has everyone thinking that anything could happen.

Rick Hutchinson, a park geologist-ranger who has earned the nickname "geyser-gazer" for his close attention to matters thermal, told us that a large mud pot near Hayden Valley had "gone wild" and was ejecting gobs of steaming muck that was coating nearby trees.

Yellowstone is a volcanic region. Subterranean volcanic magma heats the water for the springs and geysers, and much of the park lies in an immense caldera, or crater, that was created by a volcanic explosion more than half a million years ago. The caldera measures some fifty by thirty miles and includes Yellowstone Lake. Mount Sheridan forms one rim, and the other is Mount Washburn. The trail crosses the southern portion of the caldera, on high forested plateaus where wildlife is abundant.

One afternoon we hiked to the lookout atop Mount Sheridan, which, Tim Stone said, offered matchless views of the park and the Continental Divide. For hours we puffed up the rocky, relentless switchbacks, past leaking snowbanks and volcanic outcrops, to emerge at last on a windswept ridge that indeed looked and felt like the rim of a volcanic crater. We reached the top, at 10,308 feet, with the cloudy sky still turbulent in the aftermath of what veteran lookout Jim McKown called "one of the best lightning storms" he'd ever seen.

On a clear day, Jim claimed, he could see a peak 160 miles away in Idaho. Even on this cloudy afternoon we could see all of the Teton and the Absaroka Ranges and much of the Winds, the Gallatins, and the Madisons in an unobstructed sweep from the windows of the square lookout. With maps at hand, we traced the course of the Divide through the park, observed the rusty maroon area of a recent 4,800-acre forest fire northeast of Heart Lake that had been "let burn," and gauged the vastness of the Yellowstone caldera.

The views, near and far, were enchanting, and it was nearly sunset when we started back down. All of the western sky was stained with orange, and purple-gray clouds were fleeing on the wind. We picked our way down the rubbly path on the knife-edged ridge for a hundred yards, then turned. Just to the left of the lookout an enormous thunderhead, probably 30,000 feet from bottom to top, was rotating and evolving in place. Shaped roughly like an anvil, it formed and turned as if impelled by the late, warm light. From the main cloud mass, rounded blooms erupted and turned from purest white to mauve, then to pink, salmon, and orange. From the flattened underside of the anvil, lavender curtains of rain swept down to the green hills below, parted every few seconds by streaking touches of pastel lightning. The clouds, the colors, and the lightning were all reflected in the muted mirror of Heart Lake.

While we stood in awe, stunned at this enormous vision developing in complete silence, the clouds behind the lookout unveiled the pale disk of a rising full moon. Paul and I watched until the sunlight could no longer reach the anvil cloud, and the colors dimmed to dusky gray. Paul pronounced it "cosmic," and I believe now that it was the most spectacular single sight of our entire Continental Divide journey.

We then faced another, less pleasing prospect: a 2,800-foot descent through the forest after dark. We had lingered to watch the clouds and colors and lightning, and the price was several dark hours in grizzly country. Not wishing to surprise any bears, we strode down the switchbacks waving our flashlights and clapping our hands, singing and talking loudly. We must have succeeded: We reached our tents at ten o'clock, unscathed.

Wildlife abounds in Yellowstone, and the trail led us to numerous close encounters. On a stretch between Heart and Lewis Lakes, Molly and I were startled by the rushing passage of an enormous gray-brown owl. It seemed to appear from nowhere and, wings beating, ghosted over the trail at eye level and on into a pine thicket. Later I rounded a bend and met a black-coated cow moose. I was startled at her size and sudden closeness. She stood her ground astride the trail and looked me over. Then she calmly walked away.

On my last day in Yellowstone I was hiking near the geyser basin at the west end of Shoshone Lake. I had been watching a small stream, wondering how early explorers had known which rivers the streams flowed into, when I glimpsed a patch of tawny brown among the lodgepole trunks to the side of the trail — an elk. I stopped and maneuvered for a better look. Elk are a common sight along the park roads, but this one was lying alone among bushes and slender trees just thirty yards away. I stepped closer, moving deliberately, and saw that it was a mature male, with a magnificent ten-point rack of antlers. He watched me approach. The weight of his antlers gave each move of his head and neck a balanced, considered quality.

When I got to within about 15 yards of him, he rose to his feet, stared, and began browsing. He took a few steps, keeping a bush or a tree between us, and eyed me as he pulled at the greens. He had a perfectly smooth coat, all tan and brown, that grew lighter at the rump. His antlers were symmetrical and still held traces of velvet. His nose was moist and mobile and his eyes a full dark brown. I was as close as I've ever been to a full-size animal in the wild for more than a few seconds.

I was not alarmed. We stood there for a long time and looked into each other's eyes. He was rare and wild, and we gazed across a space that was at once small and unutterably vast. In that interval I wondered how the elk saw me, what impressions were collecting in his elk brain about the patchwork biped that had splashed and crackled toward him and now stood staring. He was at home, sure of his place and powers and days. We stared, and at last I backed away and turned to the trail.

Steam from Castle Geyser, perhaps the oldest active geyser in Yellowstone, obscures the setting sun. The 12-foot-high cone, resembling aged ramparts, earned the feature its name. It erupts every nine or ten hours for about an hour and a half.

Brushed by cold August fog, hikers slip and slide across the *surface of Sperry Glacier in Montana's Glacier National Park.*

IN MANY MINDS, Yellowstone is the flagship of U.S. national parks, and, like most of them, it is a difficult place to leave. It is at once so vast and so compact, and such a complete concentration of natural wonders, that you feel spoiled and bereft when the time comes to push on. But the Continental Divide is a line that always leads onward to strong experiences.

When we left the orderly park and the developments at West Yellowstone, we looked ahead to uncrowded peaks in the Centennial Mountains and in the Bitterroot Range. This would be the last leg of our trip, and I was looking forward to seeing Montana and Idaho, two states I had never visited. Half a dozen national forests, several wilderness areas, the copper country around Butte, and Glacier National Park would climax our journey.

We resumed hiking near Red Rock Pass, west of Henrys Lake in Idaho, and were surprised at how quickly we passed into wild, empty country. Atop the Centennials the Divide is mostly around 9,000 feet high, and it forms the border between Montana and Idaho. The windswept terrain is partly forested, with rocky outcrops and sweeping grassy meadows. It was good to get back up on mountains again after the lodgepole plateaus of Yellowstone National Park, and we were surprised that on beautiful weekends in August no one else was using the mountains. During one entire, perfect Saturday, we saw no other people.

The border is marked by geodetic survey markers every quarter to half a mile, and we went from one to the next, covering a westward-leading stretch in the Centennials on a day when the wind was blowing strongly out of the southwest and sending streamers of white clouds scudding just over our heads. After the storms and lightning of Colorado, we were wary of thunderclouds, so we gave some thought to dropping down the north side of the mountain to the Centennial Valley and Red Rock Lakes. The lakes were plainly visible below, surrounded by green marsh and meadows. They are a part of Red Rock Lakes National Wildlife Refuge, so, since I had been a mountain-watcher and a weather-watcher during this trip, but not yet a bird-watcher, down we went.

The refuge is a success: It was established in 1935 to protect the last of the trumpeter swans, whose number had dwindled to fewer than a hundred. The area of the refuge was an important habitat for trumpeters, and they staged a comeback that took them off the Endangered Species List in 1968. Now the 40,000-acre refuge is home to about 300 of the birds, plus many sandhill cranes and other migratory fowl. Arctic grayling live in the lakes, and other wildlife includes elk, moose, pronghorns, mule deer, white-tailed deer, coyotes, muskrats, beavers, badgers, and red foxes.

Ducks and Canada geese were swimming on the lake, and nearby

Leaving Yellowstone, the Continental Divide forms the border between Idaho and Montana for some 200 miles before angling eastward into mineral-rich mining country. Finally it turns north and completes its crossing of the U.S. in Glacier National Park.

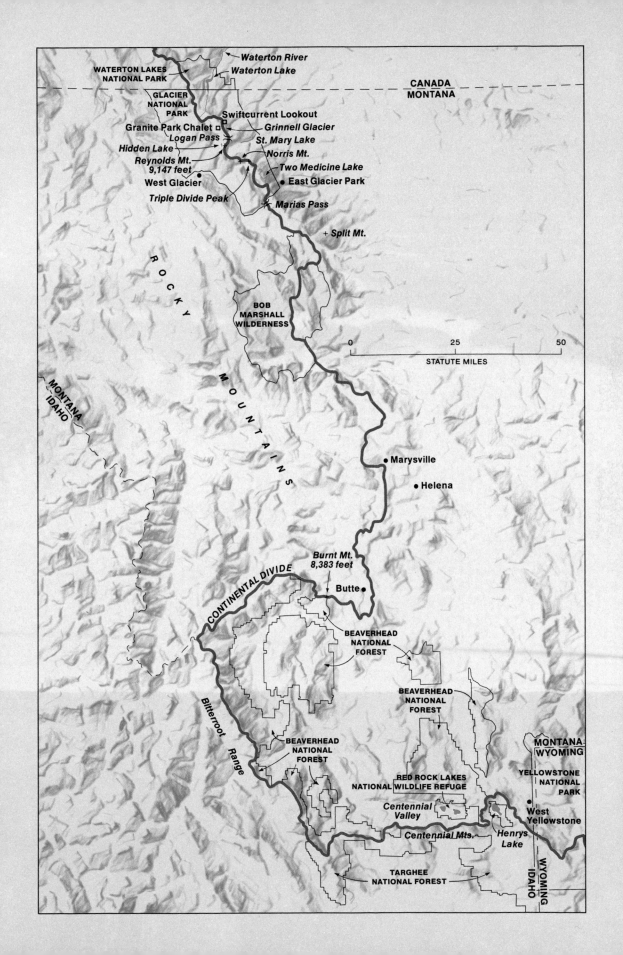

Waterton River
Waterton Lake

WATERTON LAKES
NATIONAL PARK

CANADA
MONTANA

GLACIER
NATIONAL
PARK

Swiftcurrent Lookout
Granite Park Chalet □
Grinnell Glacier
Logan Pass
St. Mary Lake
Hidden Lake
Norris Mt.
Reynolds Mt.
9,147 feet
Two Medicine Lake
West Glacier
East Glacier Park
Triple Divide Peak
Marias Pass

+ Split Mt.

R O C K Y

BOB
MARSHALL
WILDERNESS

0   25   50

STATUTE MILES

M O U N T A I N S

MONTANA
IDAHO

• Marysville

• Helena

Burnt Mt.
8,383 feet

• Butte •

CONTINENTAL DIVIDE

BEAVERHEAD
NATIONAL
FOREST

BEAVERHEAD
NATIONAL
FOREST

Bitterroot
Range

BEAVERHEAD
NATIONAL
FOREST

MONTANA
WYOMING

YELLOWSTONE
NATIONAL
PARK

RED ROCK LAKES
NATIONAL WILDLIFE REFUGE

Centennial
Valley

• West
Yellowstone

Centennial Mts.

Henrys
Lake

WYOMING
IDAHO

TARGHEE
NATIONAL FOREST

Summer adds a stroke of green to the Red Rock Lakes National Wildlife Refuge. Snowmelt from the Centennial Mountains feeds the marshes and the clear blue lakes that lace this 40,000-acre Montana preserve. Created in 1935 as a sanctuary for endangered trumpeter swans, the refuge provides a home for increasing numbers of trumpeters, as well as other wildlife. At right, red foxes sun themselves near their den.

147

I saw a western grebe (and waited in vain for its spectacular, walking-on-water mating dance), an American kestrel, whistling swans, trumpeter swans, mergansers, a great blue heron, and a small rail.

Gene Stroops, the manager of the refuge, came here from Benton, Montana. He told me that, though there are no maintained trails and no visitor center, the refuge is open to the public. "Mostly we get fly-fishermen," he said, "coming over here from Yellowstone for the grayling." It is an out-of-the-way place, and I noticed that the power and telephone lines stopped at the refuge. "Yes," said Gene, "there are ranches for another thirty or forty miles up the Centennial Valley, past the lines, but it's a pretty isolated life up there. Especially after the snow falls." Near the refuge, we had passed some derelict ranch houses with grass growing up to their windowsills. The unpainted buildings had gone to silver with the passing seasons. I had seen enough working ranches by now to know that unceasing sweat and labor must be expended to keep them going. These quiet skeletal buildings seemed testimony not only to isolation, but also to effort, to lively hopes worked out and then withdrawn. This end of Montana looked like classic ranch country, the kind I'd been seeing in movies all my life, but these shriveled, dry buildings told of a life that seldom makes the movies.

Some surprising snowfalls in August drove us out of the Bitterroot high country, down from the string of pure, cold lakes just downwind from the Divide, and we looked ahead to lower forests, into the lodgepoles again.

Montana is heavily wooded in its western end, and much of the proposed Continental Divide Trail—except in the upper elevations of Glacier National Park—tracks along through almost continuous forest. Conifers predominate, especially the lodgepole pine in the southern and central parts of the state. It is everywhere, perhaps because it is one of the quickest species to fill the void left by fire. It needs the high temperature of a fire to open its small, prickled cones and to spread its seeds. That fact also seems to account for the lodgepole's gregariousness; we nearly always found it growing in crowds of its own kind, the tall straight trunks massed in a way that made me think I was seeing the forest but not the trees. It is happiest on dry slopes in elevations of five to ten thousand feet, where most other species don't grow. This aptly describes the zone of western Montana cut by the Continental Divide.

However, the forests of Montana are under siege, and we were to see the casualties all the way to the Canadian border: the characteristic dead-brown bodies of trees slain by the pine bark beetle.

"The lodgepole is most readily damaged," spokesman Jed Dewey told us at a forest service regional office in Missoula. "Of course the beetles do attack and kill others, like the limber, the whitebark, and the ponderosa pines." The siege began a few years ago. It's an outbreak that is expected to last another ten years or so, during which time it will kill some 80 percent of the trunks that are more than nine inches in diameter. That includes much of the lodgepole-pine forest of western Montana.

Paul and I toured the office's lab, which is devoted to gathering information about insect infestations. "The beetles are always there," Jed explained. "Even though cold weather slows them down, and fire kills them. They begin to multiply—and become a problem—when there's been no interruption by a fire or a harvest, or when a substantial number of trees get to be more than eighty years old or more than eight inches in diameter. Then the beetles' food supply—they feed on the phloem, the soft conductive tissue under the bark—becomes ample. And they multiply."

Is there any way to stop the beetles? I asked, thinking of the dismal prospect of a forest 80 percent dead. "The real hope lies in silviculture," Jed said, "the mixing of trees, the diversification of ages and species. And in good management, which includes harvesting trees so you don't get large uniform stands of, say, lodgepole pines all the same age. Spraying can protect individual high-value trees for up to two years, but this is only feasible in such areas as campgrounds, not in large forested areas. There's not much we can do in the wilderness areas." So for the next decade, it seems, backpackers along the Continental Divide will be camping some of the time under brown, lifeless lodgepoles.

Trees were being harvested when I hiked the section of trail that loops out of the Bitterroots and points east and north toward copper country. Near Deer Lodge Pass, heading toward Burnt Mountain, I passed around and through several squared-off sections that had been clear-cut. Trees had been felled, trimmed, and the boles hauled away on those enormous logging trucks that make back-roads driving here such an adventure. Only stumps, light slash, and quantities of sawdust remained—nothing to impede the growth of the next generation of lodgepoles, which were already past seedling stage.

This was an area to try my patience and my navigational skills. Nothing around me, for miles at a time, seemed to correspond to the lines on my map. One of us had to be wrong. But whether I was on the right track or not, the trails were easy walking. They crossed dry, upland terrain with ridges and plateaus and flats, with the mountains spread out for good viewing but not grouped as constant obstacles. This is the kind of area where the Continental Divide seems especially to be only an idea in the mind of fugitive map makers.

West central Montana, along the Divide, is copper country, and the history of the mineral's extraction is on view all over the dry brown slopes, in the ghost towns, and at the World Museum of Mining —a collection of mining hardware in Butte. Butte itself seems perpetually about to slide into the maw of Berkeley Pit, a vast hole that was begun above a vein of low-grade copper in 1954.

"We move about 50,000 tons of ore a day," explained Rick Ramseier, the personable chief geologist of the Anaconda Copper Company. "But it's only .6 percent copper, so we get only about 12 pounds of copper per ton of ore. It's all part of the Boulder Batholith, a relatively young intrusion of rocks ranging from gabbro to granite. Butte's on the southwestern end of it, and it extends roughly to Helena. There are many other interesting geological features in the area, but of course," he smiled, "it's the one we're interested in.

Outfitter Phil Wright mans the net as his wife, Joan, reels in an 18-inch rainbow trout from the Big Hole River in Montana. Oliver, their yellow Labrador retriever, appears eager to help. At upper left, Phil removes a barbless hook from a brook trout. "We release nearly all the fish we catch," says Phil, "and always the big ones; they make the best brood stock." Known nationally for his expertise in fly-fishing, Phil demonstrates the art of tying a fly. Wrapping nylon thread around a chicken feather, he creates an imitation stone fly, also called a salmon fly for its orange color. Elk hairs conceal the hook. At lunchtime (left), Joan spreads a picnic at riverside.

151

Copper mining will go on here for at least another twenty years; we're going to resume deep mining soon. Gold and silver were discovered here in the 1860s, but no one's mining them significantly now. Copper wasn't extensively mined here until the turn of the century, when the demand for electrical power transmission developed."

North of Butte we stopped at some of the mining sites and ghost towns on the Divide. Near Blossburg, in dry brown hills, we saw how formidable a barrier the Divide can be, even in these comparatively low mountains: Out of the mouth of Mullan Tunnel, next to a sign that read "Continental Divide. el. 5,548 feet," labored a long Burlington-Northern freight train, its multiple green-and-white diesel engines throbbing and smoking. The train had crept westward on lines that looped and curved to gain elevation, and then passed under the Divide. The crew waved to us and to the section hands who stood aside to watch its passage.

Marysville is just off the Divide in a narrow valley surrounded by pine-covered hills and bluffs. It ranks as one of the best mining ghost towns I've seen. We walked its six streets and found most of its forty or so buildings occupied. There was one church steeple and one active business—the Marysville House Saloon—which hadn't yet opened for the day. It was a cool morning, and a friendly St. Bernard fell in with us and tagged along.

Ghost towns, if they are as accessible as Marysville, survive precariously. If many of the log cabins, false-front stores, and stone or brick mining buildings are still in good shape, people who crave solitude move in. Such towns soon begin to draw tourists, and as the traffic grows, businesses begin catering to the tourists, and the town starts getting fixed up. The popular ones seem to hit a flash point and explode into ski resorts or theme parks or masses of boutiques, and the ghost is gone. Like wilderness areas, ghost towns sometimes get loved to death.

The proposed Continental Divide Trail enters Glacier National Park from the southeast, near the point where the Continental Divide itself crosses Marias Pass, a mile-high opening to the west traversed by a transcontinental railroad. It's an entry Paul and I had been looking forward to from the start, as a climax and a final recapitulation of everything that is great about hiking along the Continental Divide. Glacier has 1,583 square miles of wilderness, spectacularly varied scenery, climbable mountains, genuine glaciers, comfortable chalets, accessible wildlife, excellent trails, and enthusiastic outdoor people, including some of the "hikingest" park rangers we met. The high forested trail leads from Marias Pass to East Glacier Park—one of two Amtrak stops near the park—and then north, arcing along Two Medicine Lake and across Pitamakan Pass. There the trail closely coincides with the Divide itself. On this humid morning, we were hiking north of Pitamakan to a unique point: Triple Divide Peak, where the waters drain to three oceans.

"It's a hiker's park, a backpacker's paradise," veteran seasonal ranger Wyatt Woodsmall assured me. We were following the narrow, damp trail from Cut Bank Ranger Station, and Wyatt's quick pace left me with insufficient wind to do more than answer him in monosyllabic grunts. But he was able to sustain a running monologue on the park's trails while we hiked along watching eastbound clouds for curtains of rain and the cow parsnip patches for signs of grizzly bears.

Before World War II many park visitors were on horseback. "You'd have as many as 500 head of horses coming through here in the '20s and early '30s," Wyatt said as we hiked upward along the flank of Mount James. "They'd get off the train at East Glacier Park and ride from tent camp to chalet, all through here." The trail slanted upward above the wooded valley of Atlantic Creek, which flows eastward out of Medicine Grizzly Lake. A wave of rain clouds passed over, wetting us on the outside while we sweated inside rain jackets and ponchos. "There was a chalet at Cut Bank, another at St. Mary, and another at Two Medicine Lake. The camp store at Two Med"—where I'd had a cup of hot chocolate — "used to be a chalet. President Roosevelt delivered his very first fireside chat from there. But they tore a lot of chalets down around the time of World War II. They were falling down anyway, and visitation had dropped off. The ones at Sperry and Granite Park are all that are left."

We entered a narrow stretch of trail where thick, high vegetation limited our visibility. Wyatt answered my questioning look: "Yes, this is good grizzly habitat ... open area with plenty of food ... cow parsnip and lots of berries. There're ground squirrels here, and it's close to water. Perfect," he concluded. We hiked on, scanning the trail ahead and talking loudly.

It is impossible—and undesirable—to hike in Glacier National Park without thinking about grizzly bears, even though it's unlikely that a hiker will encounter any of the park's estimated 200 resident grizzlies. It's just that they can be dangerous if surprised, and the park personnel can never forget the six campers who have been mauled to death here by grizzlies since 1967.

There is no simple, comforting answer to the question of what to do when you meet a grizzly. North America's preeminent omnivore, the grizzly may grow eight feet tall, weigh 600 pounds, and eat anything. Grizzlies can run faster than you can—no matter who you are—have been known to climb trees, can brain a moose with a single swipe, fear nothing, and are not stupid. They see fairly well but depend more on their excellent sense of smell. They are very curious, so they sometimes rush right up to an object—a quaking backpacker, for example—just to see what it is. So what to do? We were told: Keep a very clean camp, and don't eat while hiking. Make a lot of noise in bear habitat. Stay alert. If confronted, stop and talk softly to the bear while retreating to the nearest tall tree. Then climb, quickly. You mustn't run; bears are like dogs, and if you run they'll chase you. Consider dropping your pack as a diversion. Make no aggressive moves, no thrusts with your Swiss Army knife. If all else fails, fall to the ground, cover your neck, and play dead. Prayer is optional. Seasonal ranger Richard Gustason was photographing wild flowers in an open meadow when he was surprised by an approaching grizzly only yards away. Richard played dead, and the grizzly simply stepped over his outstretched arms.

Gaping mile-wide Berkeley Pit, mined by the Anaconda Copper Company, creeps

toward the outskirts of Butte. One ton of material here yields about 12 pounds of copper.

155

When we reached Triple Divide Pass—elevation 7,410 feet—the falling rain dimmed our view and forced us under a nearby outcrop for a dry lunch. We sat overlooking Split Mountain and the valley of Hudson Bay Creek, sharing sandwich halves, peaches, orange sections, and gorp — a mixture of nuts, seeds, and dried fruit. Wyatt explained the geology of the park area: "All of Glacier National Park was once at the bottom of shallow seas, which deposited layers of sedimentary rock. The red rock—which seems to be the most prominent rock in the park—is Grinnell argillite. It's got iron compounds in it, and from time to time when it was raised out of the water it rusted. The green rock you see"—a rich jade color—"is Appekunny argillite. It was deeper and never exposed to air, so it never rusted." Visible in the adjacent mountains and around us at the pass was a lighter, almost white band of rock—marble. An igneous intrusion of magma occurred deep underground here, long before the mountains were uplifted. It was so hot it metamorphosed the limestone above and below it, forming two layers of white marble. The dark diorite band between them is about 110 feet thick and is seen in most of the great cliff faces near the Continental Divide. The thinner white bands are always visible above and below it. Indeed, as we were to see, marble runs through the park near the Continental Divide like the white line down the center of a highway.

Wyatt Woodsmall is an experienced climber, so, when the rain tapered off after lunch, we decided to hike as high as we could up Triple Divide Peak. It is a ridge of the larger Norris Mountain and, at 8,011 feet, it's not a tough climb.

We climbed steadily and slowly, carefully seeking secure handholds among the brittle layers of sedimentary rock. Glacier is not a classic climber's park. It is, rather, notorious as a place where you "have to hold the rocks together as you climb." Wyatt said: "This is the only triple divide watershed in North America, for the Atlantic, the Pacific, and for Hudson Bay." We strolled around the summit and looked down into the three creeks. The rain that had been falling on this rocky surface was already on its way to three great bodies of water a continent apart. We stood above timberline, and visibility was about 75 miles, enough to see the sunlight glowing on wheatfields in Alberta. The Continental Divide was a vivid reality. We could see water flashing on all three sides. Rain was still falling far out in the three drainages. When we reached the summit of Norris, the sky had cleared, so we were treated to a full-circle view of mountains: Little Chief, Almost-a-Dog, Split, and Red Eagle, and the glacial valley down to St. Mary Lake, sparkling now in the afternoon sun. We stood in the pale sun right on the knife-edge. As is usual when atop a mountain, we wanted to stay. No one wanted to start back down.

Granite Park Chalet is a big, (Continued on page 162)

Relics of former days, abandoned buildings line the main street of Marysville, once a gold-mining town. In the late 1800s this business district catered to a population of several thousand people.

CONTINENTAL DIVIDE
BELMONT SKI AREA
OPHIR CREEK

Sheep scatter across a grassy hillside as shepherd Luke Mickels keeps a protective eye on them. Luke tends 1,600 of the animals for the Sieben Ranch near Lincoln. With his flock grazing close to camp, Luke finds time for a bath (far left). His wife, Julie, replenishes the hot water. "It's a simple life," says Luke, "and I love it."

FOLLOWING PAGES: Morning light burnishes a limestone escarpment 1,000 feet high that forms the Divide for 12 miles in the Bob Marshall Wilderness in northwestern Montana.

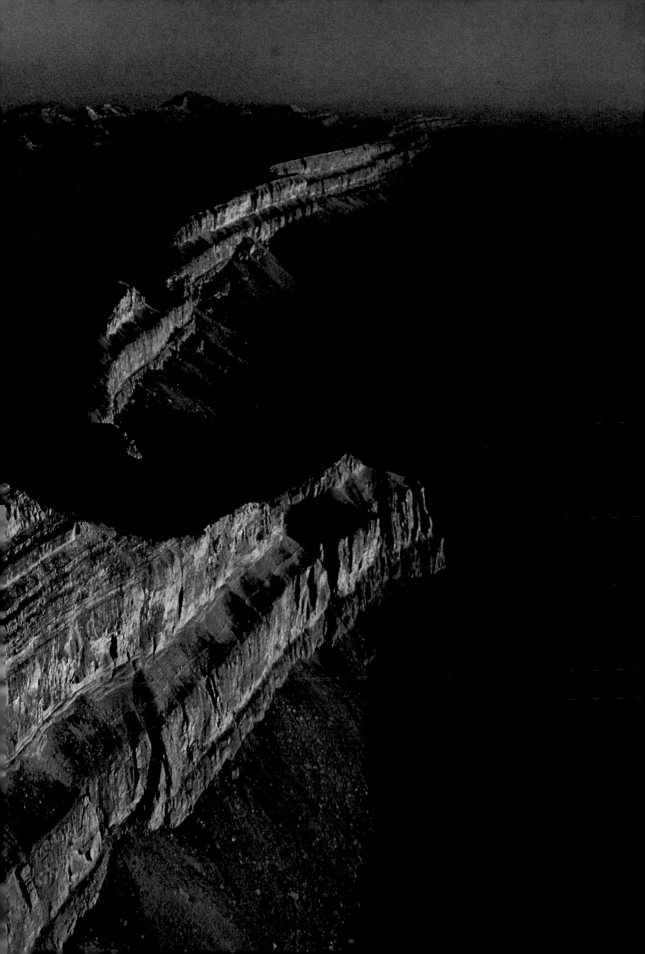

North America's only three-way watershed, pyramid-shaped Triple Divide Peak (foreground) sends water runoff to three oceans: the Atlantic, the Pacific, and the Arctic via Hudson Bay.

rustic, foursquare structure, built with stone quarried near the site. The choice rooms upstairs, facing the balconies, sleep four or eight, and the rooms in the smaller, newer stone annex are similarly arranged. On the Highline Trail from Logan Pass hikers parallel the Divide on the Pacific side, with opportunities to spot nimble white mountain goats far overhead and to see the chalet for several miles of more-or-less level trail before arriving.

The chalet is a romantic, rare place to stay, a respite from nylon tents and meals on the ground. It is European in flavor and offers nothing to do except eat and sleep and hike and talk. Meals are taken in an "everything" room—with picnic tables, old cards and magazines, a fireplace, and a wood-burning stove with places for drying boots and jeans. Meals are served with alacrity by an ebullient—if somewhat cabin-fevered—staff of undergraduates.

I slept soundly on a log-framed double-deck bed, with welcome wool blankets, but was surprised at the noise level in such a remote place. The interior partition walls are leaf thin, so a communal air prevails, even at bedtime. The real surprise was the racket that erupted in the darkest, stillest part of the night. I snapped awake to listen to heavy scrabbling outside. Some animal digging, I thought, and slept again. The next morning it was clear that a bear had been excavating in pursuit of small burrowing animals and had dug up some bear-size heaps of dirt and gravel. Bears again!

There have always been bears around the Granite Park Chalet and animal-watching—bears, goats, deer, ground squirrels—is the favored after-dinner recreation. It was at the campground just below the chalet that a fatal mauling occurred in 1967. After seeing the quantities of earth moved and checking on the insubstantial door that had separated my bedroom from the diligent bear, I decided it was time to learn more about *Ursus arctos horribilis.*

"The proposed Continental Divide Trail goes through some mighty good grizzly bear country," I was assured in jovial tones. I had sought out one of the park's resident authorities, research biologist Cliff Martinka. Cliff had been involved with bears ("They shaped my career") since 13 years before, when, as a young biologist, he was part of a team that successfully pursued some rogue grizzlies. Now he chases hard facts about bears, about bear-human encounters, about changes in bear behavior. He likes to plot his findings on maps.

"Our data suggest that bear problems may be increasing," he explained. His map of bear-human contacts—there are 300 to 500 grizzly sightings a year—nearly coincides with the park's map showing the most heavily visited areas. "The problem is that after a lot of contact a bear begins to lose its shyness. It begins seeing more people, maybe starts charging and getting hikers to drop their backpacks." So the park is now grappling with the question of how many more people can be tolerated in the grizzly habitats. The park's signs and pamphlets make it clear that the bears were here first, that this was *their* habitat first, and that hikers enter these areas at their own risk. How great is that risk? I asked Cliff if he would sleep out at the Granite Park campground now. He said he would not.

After two fatal maulings in 1967, changes were made in park policy in an attempt—not entirely successful, as it turned out—to forestall further killings. Before 1967, garbage was sometimes fed to the grizzlies at Granite Park. Campgrounds were not policed and were trashy. Backcountry users camped anywhere, and there was little effort to educate them about bears and the simple steps that mitigate the danger, like tying food inaccessibly high above and some distance away from an overnight campsite. Now the numbers of overnight users are limited. Camping is permitted mostly at designated sites and times, and the campgrounds are patrolled by rangers. All trash must be packed out. At the time *(Continued on page 169)*

Veteran mountaineer Dr. J. Gordon Edwards leads climbers along a rubble-strewn

ridge to the 9,147-foot summit of Reynolds Mountain in Glacier National Park.

With Bearhat Mountain and Hidden Lake behind and below them, Mike and his
15-year-old daughter, Molly, backpack in Glacier National Park. Established in
1910, the million-acre park quickly gained renown as a hiker's paradise. Today nearly
600 miles of trails cross prairie meadows, rim snow-fed lakes, skirt rumbling glaciers,
and climb through conifer forests to treeless, windswept peaks. At right, Mike and
Molly stop to examine some of nature's small splendors: alpine wild flowers in colorful
profusion. Camping beside Hidden Lake, Molly snuggles into her sleeping bag to ward
off the evening chill as her father cooks dinner.

you register for a campsite, you must read pamphlets about bears and sign a statement that the warnings were read (and heard, as there is a question-and-answer period) and understood. The gravity of the matter is impressed on all who use this wilderness, and it seems appreciated: Most of the hikers we met were wearing bells or other noisemakers, kept very clean camps, and were well aware of bear presence and bear signs.

Still, further tragedies occurred. A young woman was killed at Many Glacier Campground in September of 1976 when she tried to photograph a grizzly. A young man and woman were both killed while camped near St. Mary one dreadful night in July 1980. The body of a Texas man, mauled and partially eaten, was found in October.

"Normally," Charles Jonkel of the University of Montana told us, "bears are afraid of people." Charles had been described to us as a "world authority on bears" by Cliff Martinka. "They'll just treat you like a superbear. Then, after a while, they lose their fear of people. They start exploiting people. They find out that people have food. Then they find out that people *are* food." Charles loves and respects bears ("I never hunt bears; it'd be like hunting family") and is now engaged in field research on how a disturbance—a disruption of its environment, for instance — affects a bear's behavior. He and his associates are tracking twenty or so radio-equipped bears. "Most of the disturbing incidents occur in the national parks, where a lot of people are present in the bears' habitat." Occasionally Charles is called upon to help remove a problem bear to a new environment, usually in remote areas of British Columbia.

He is concerned that the proposed Continental Divide Trail may go too near the denning areas above 7,500 feet that the bears favor. "They dig in and fix things up, build a chamber with a sill and everything. Then they bring in about five or six bushels of beargrass for bedding and close off the entrance. Their heart rate goes down to one or two beats a minute, but their temperature doesn't drop much. They are quite vulnerable then, for six or seven months."

When we had first approached Granite Park Chalet, striding north on the Highline Trail, an afternoon storm was gathering over the western ridges. We had enjoyed weeks of sunny skies and now, as we hiked around a long level cirque with a clear view of the chalet, we watched as storm clouds piled up darkly and began changing the mountains to monochrome blue silhouettes, the valley to a deeper green. The clouds advanced, turned silver, then roiled purple at the edges. To the north, pale curtains of rain swept across the Divide. We raced to reach the shelter of the chalet.

We panted onto its stone porch just in time to hear the supper gong, and just as the first cold drops splatted onto our packs. Mixed feelings in a dangerously dry season: The rain would dampen the forest tinder, but the storm would bring lightning strikes—and fire.

Skidding wildly, Mike whoops as he glissades down a snowfield near Hidden Lake; Molly takes a running start. In Glacier, snow survives on high mountaintops throughout the summer months.

No one viewed the coming storm with more ambivalence than the first man we met at the chalet: Brian Stricker, the resident lookout of nearby Swiftcurrent Mountain and one of the few people who live exactly atop the Continental Divide. Fire-watching from a tower is on the wane: It's easier to keep an eye on forests from airplanes, and it's getting harder to find people willing to man the mountaintop stations. So after supper, when twilight rain was gusting onto the windows and Brian announced he was going to climb the two-mile, 1,700-foot ascent back to the lookout on the peak of Swiftcurrent, I asked if I might go along and stay through the stormy night.

We set off in darkness with the rain coming down from the eastbound storm overhead. "We'd better hurry," Brian warned. "The alpine section of this trail is no place to be when lightning strikes." On the steep, empty switchbacks above the treeline, the storm overtook us, the horizontal wind pushing at our faces, then at our backs, then our faces again. The rain struck like a stream of cold needles. To the south and west behind us, strong shots of lightning split the night. Brian warned me, shouting over the wind: "If you feel 'signs' — tingling, or your hair standing up—head for the bottom. We'll be okay once we're on top; everything's insulated." No electricity touched us, but the storm clouds poured around us, obscuring the pinpoint lights below. Without Brian to follow, I'd have lost the trail a dozen times in the darkness. Wet and chilled, we reached the lantern-lit lookout cabin in fifty minutes.

Brian anticipated my question: "The wind never stops." It blustered and flared, bowing mournful music from the guy wires. It made the roof crackle and distorted the reflecting windows. We sat and listened, watching in dimness as the ragged clouds flowed over the Divide, and lightning feelers touched the dark mountains below. The "Swiftie" lookout is a 14-by-14-foot wooden cabin built in 1936 on a stone foundation. At each corner it is secured by a half-inch steel cable grouted into the mountain rock. On the roof there are three lightning rods with cables that lead to the ground. Brian hadn't yet experienced a direct lightning hit this season.

The storm rolled east toward the flatland, and one lightning strike ignited an orange flare-up on Flattop Mountain some 12 miles away. Brian checked it with binoculars, then sighted in with a fire-finder. With a combination of azimuth reading, vertical angle reading, and a visual cross-check with a topographic map, he determined the fire's location and radioed it to the park service dispatcher at West Glacier. After twenty minutes the fire went out, apparently extinguished by the cold rain.

"This is a great place to watch the light change," Brian told me. "There have been some incredible sunrises and sunsets. I often wake to see the sun come up; it's hard to sleep once it's up." Brian also has seen some odd and unexplained flashes of light during the day, and at night, meteor showers, satellites, and the aurora borealis. "You slow down enough to see things here," he said. "It's good for getting to know yourself. There's nothing here to keep you from yourself."

Brian, just 20, is an adventurer. He has worked in other mountains and in an Alaskan cannery and was planning a trip to the Himalayas after the lookout closed for the season. We found that we were both reading the same book just then, Peter Matthiessen's *The Snow Leopard*. Brian wants to go to Tibet and Nepal because he "loves mountains," and to "see the Himalayas before they change."

"Coming here was the best thing I could have done," he said, and added that he was considering returning for the next season.

On the clearest days Brian can see past the mountains across the flatlands to the Sweet Grass Hills eighty to ninety miles away in eastern Montana. The storm passed that way during the night.

In the morning I was denied any view: The storm had left behind a fog so complete the windows looked painted white. Brian rose early, nonetheless, and started making pancakes and coffee. In my sleeping bag on the floor I noticed for the first time that each leg of Brian's steel bedstead was fitted with a large glass insulator.

The mountain views from the trail in Glacier National Park are equal to any along the Divide, despite their comparatively modest elevation. Usually the trail is close to the Divide itself, which is often a forbidding succession of sawtooth peaks and impossible vertical drops trod only by mountain goats. But it does sometimes coincide with peaks that are possible, climbable, and offer great views. Reynolds Mountain, for example.

"Rock!" Sally Taylor, a park summer employee and student from Alabama, shouted the warning as a shoe-size chunk of argillite broke loose and tumbled. Everyone froze or ducked except Jane Edwards, who fielded it as deftly as a shortstop and set it aside, to the relief of those below. Loose rock, a climbing hazard anywhere, is a special, constant concern to people scrambling up the crumbling sedimentary layers of Glacier's mountains.

Twelve of us, a pickup party, had been climbing the Logan Pass approach of 9,147-foot Reynolds Mountain for two hours and were ascending a ladder-steep chute that led onto the spectacular "goat trail." This foot-wide track—it sometimes seemed no more than a deep scratch in the rock—traverses the north face of the mountain. It is visible as a faint line from far below at the Logan Pass visitor center. Reynolds is not a difficult mountain, but I noticed our party stayed quite close together and close to the vertical wall on the right. At my shoulder this sheer rise—up and out of sight—was decorated with patterns of white, pale-green, and pumpkin-orange lichens. Off to my left, just past my carefully placed boot, a slope of scree slanted down at a 45-degree angle for about ten feet to an edge, the cornice of a straight drop-off of several hundred feet. My daughter, Molly, who had enjoyed some rock-climbing in Wyoming, said over her shoulder that she was "apprehensive but not scared." A fine and useful distinction, I thought, and reminded her not to look down.

Our route had been selected *(Continued on page 182)*

FOLLOWING PAGES: *Rising from the mist like a restless sea, the Rockies crest in wavelike peaks. Glaciers carved the long, narrow valleys, and erosion works ceaselessly to dull the summits.*

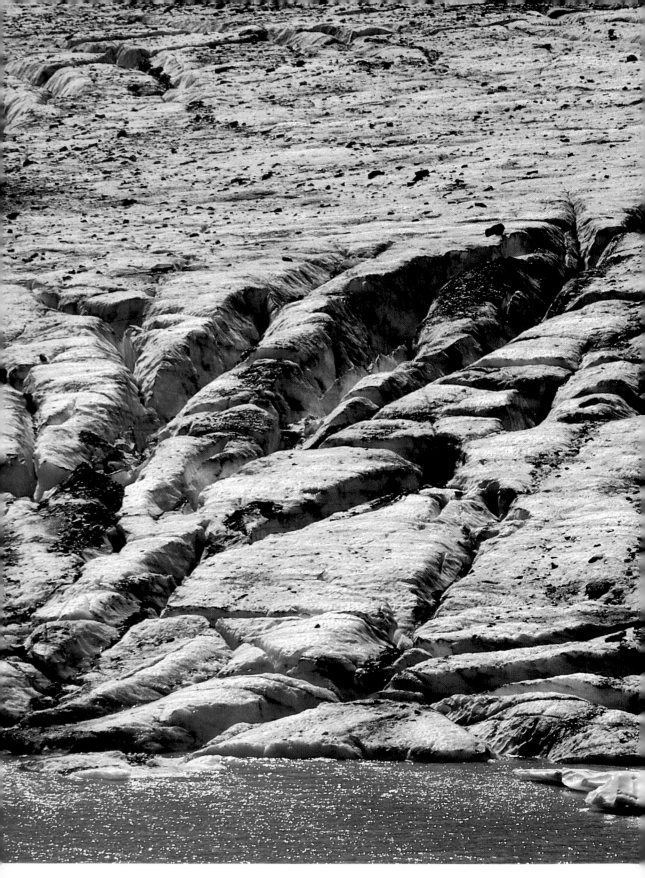

Crevasses scar the massive face of Grinnell Glacier. Largest of the park's

forty glaciers, this slow-moving bed of ice covers nearly 300 acres.

Backpackers hit the trail after a stop at Granite Park Chalet, one of two lodges in Glacier that offer hikers hot food and bunks. These two Ohio State University students spent a week hiking in the park. Even in rain and fog the wilderness beckons (opposite). Janel Crabtree, draped in improvised rain gear, says: "Glacier has its own special beauty, and the best way to see it is to put a pack on your back and walk."

FOLLOWING PAGES: Reduced to specks by a massive cliff, hikers creep along the Highline Trail in Glacier. Though less dangerous than it looks, this section of the popular 34-mile trail nevertheless has steel cables bolted to the rocks for handrails.

H ackles rising, a feeding grizzly glares a warning: Stay away! Powerful and unpredictable, grizzlies lose their normal shyness as contact with people increases. They have mauled and killed six campers in the park since it opened in 1910, three in 1980 alone. Trailside posters (above) alert hikers to bear habitats. Grizzlies use the leaves of beargrass (below) to line their winter dens.

by Dr. J. Gordon Edwards, a tanned, athletic professor at California's San Jose State University. We could scarcely have been in better company: Edwards literally wrote the book on climbing in Glacier National Park. He is a veteran of the U.S. Army's legendary Tenth Mountain Division, where David Brower, of the Sierra Club and Friends of the Earth, was his commanding officer. Dr. Edwards was a seasonal ranger in Glacier for nine seasons and climbed every major mountain in the park. He had first climbed Reynolds Mountain 32 years before. "It's a climb of three to four hours," he observed at the start. "And it's a safe mountain; no one has ever died on Reynolds. It is," he added, "my favorite in the park."

Our route took us all around the mountain, starting at lush alpine meadows in Logan Pass, which is directly on the Continental Divide. Dr. Edwards and Jean Crouch, of Oakton, Virginia, took turns identifying wild flowers for us: Saint-John's-wort, with bright orange buds; arnica, "the bigger yellow flowers"; monkey flowers, "tubular, pink, or purple"; purple asters; and grass-of-parnassus, the "five-petal white ones, with the grassy center." Our brisk hike was witnessed by mountain goats and an occasional ptarmigan and signaled by marmots whistling among the outcrops.

From the meadow we followed a long open ridge on the Divide, then up a steeper ridge, across some talus and up the chutes that led to the goat trail. After lunch we traversed downward over loose scree on the east side. This was the faintest stretch of trail, where it was clear to everyone that if you slipped on the scree you'd be gone. Gordon cautioned us to get our weight uphill, so that lost footing would mean no more than abruptly sitting down in place.

After scaling some chimneys and successive ledges, we slanted up the southwestern side to what Gordon called the magic ledge, which led to the last steps up onto the narrow summit ridge.

The wind blew during the entire climb, punctuating our talk with the click-clack of falling rocks: the slow-motion sound of a mountain tumbling down. The wind was cold, and a storm moved slowly toward us from the west, bringing a ceiling of solid gray clouds that dropped lower and lower during our climb. At the top they seemed within arm's reach overhead. The passing sweeps of faint rain turned once or twice to snow that swirled around us—on the afternoon of August 15!

On the summit we signed the register that was concealed in a cairn. We leaned into the wind and were scanning a 360-degree panorama of Glacier's mountains—Fusillade, Citadel, Siyeh, Bishops Cap—when Molly lost a contact lens she'd been cleaning. On hands and knees, we all searched among the rock chips, joking about cleaning off the entire mountaintop, until Molly managed to find it. But it was too scratched and battered to use, so Molly made the tricky descent of Reynolds with one eye shut.

Another tricky descent—probably the trickiest I ever experienced —occurred a short time later near Granite Park Chalet. I got a lasting lesson in how easy it is to get in trouble when I violated one of my own rules: Never hike or climb alone in rugged terrain.

It happened during a solitary climb from the Highline Trail to the notched crags on the Divide above the chalet. After a pleasant morning's climb and a peaceful lunch, I began my descent from the ridge. I took a shortcut toward what appeared to be a likely junction with the trail, but found myself at the edge of a drop-off, a cliff I hadn't realized was there; it separated me from the trail. The total drop was about a hundred feet, but there were ledges running downward, with trees, chimneys, and handhold cracks—almost a trail. I could backtrack a mile or so and hike off the saddle on the other side, or I could climb down this cliff. Without much thought, I decided to climb down.

I picked out what appeared to be a continuous succession of holds and ledges that led in a distinct traverse across to a chimney that would allow an easy descent. But about halfway down I got stymied. I'd been moving along a narrowing ledge until I came to a long stretch from one foothold to the next where I could find no adequate handhold. It wasn't a gap I could leap; the footing was too precarious. Already I had stooped and stretched just to reach this point, and had felt some of those infamous sedimentary layers crumble away. I was not certain that I could simply retrace my steps to the top.

So I stood a long time, examining the possibilities. A forty-foot fall onto edged boulders was no joke. I reviewed what I knew about climbing, about climbing *alone*, about overconfidence, about route selection. I would have to make a move soon, before I got nervous or careless or fatigued. I chose a likely combination of not entirely satisfactory handholds, and made my move: a long step, left hand to a good grippy outcrop, right hand under a ledge, then right hand to a rock point and a reach around with the left into a cleft in the rock. With my left hand secure in a good grip, I stretched fully to the next foothold, but my left grip wasn't so secure after all: When my weight hit it, the rocks came loose in my hand. I held tight with just my right hand and foot as dislodged rocks showered onto me. When they stopped pulling loose and falling, I was crouched on one foot, balanced against the cliff with a boulder the size of an anvil in my lap, along with a dozen or so rocks the size of hiking shoes. I found myself, then, in serious trouble. And suddenly, on this bright warm day, I felt very alone and careless.

Charged with adrenalin, I waited a moment to calm down, then carefully began picking up and dropping the smaller rocks until the anvil was all I had to contend with. I couldn't slip it past my legs without risking loss of balance and a fall. So I wedged it back into the crack it had come from. It fit solidly enough to stay but not to hold onto. With the sequence of handholds altered, it then appeared that my best chance lay in turning around, shifting my feet, and stretching with my right leg to a ledge by the chimney. But, wedged against the cliff, I couldn't turn with my bulky pack still on my back. I reached and unclipped it, mentally checked the contents for anything breakable, and let it go. I expected it to fall only the forty feet to the boulders and talus below, and stop. Instead it fell, hit, and rolled and tumbled some 400 feet down the talus slope. It looked like a small body as it bounded end over end in the sunlight. I watched it until it stopped, and wondered if I'd do that if I fell.

So I moved very steadily, turned and changed feet on the narrow ledge, changed my hand grips, and without looking down or anywhere except at the target foothold, stretched five feet to safety. Once on the ledge, I continued in a quick, simple descent. I retrieved my pack—somewhat scuffed by its long tumble—and sat for a while in the sun on the solid ground and thought about carelessness and luck and climbing lessons. It's very easy to get in trouble.

There are several dozen glaciers in the park, and many of them are clustered along the Continental Divide. They are peculiar objects, though not so dramatic as the towering, creeping, blue-ice glaciers seen elsewhere. Here they are masses of gray or blue ice, often spread in a semicircle in an alpine cirque or in the lee shadow of a peak. To the summer visitor they are indistinguishable from a permanent snowfield, and indeed they are often covered all year by snow. But a glacier is defined as a permanent ice mass, formed by accumulations of snow, no less than one hundred feet thick, that moves at least ten feet a year, and the glaciers here meet that definition.

They have some unnerving characteristics that make them hazardous attractions. They boom and shake with the freezing and thawing, with the sunlight and nightfall, and with the cracking and advancing that is always occurring. A crevasse can open suddenly, with the report of a cannon. Or one may lie in wait, thinly skinned with a deceptive snowbridge. Visitors are advised to avoid the park's snow-covered glaciers unless they are accompanied by a ranger or a naturalist, but they sometimes go anyway. So the rangers must always be ready for a rescue.

Rescue gear is permanently stowed in fifty-gallon steel drums at major glaciers that are accessible to visitors. The gear includes climbing ropes, carabiners, blankets, crampons, and hard hats. Because rescue teams have to hurry, they are helicoptered to the glaciers.

It would be easy to stay indefinitely in Glacier; it's one of those places that cannot be exhausted, where every stride changes the light and the view and adds to your store of wilderness experience. But at last it was time to move north to the Canadian border. We left the chalet and followed the trail along a sweeping series of grand cirques with the Divide overhead and the hazy green valley of Mineral Creek, full of pointed dark firs, on our left.

Near Ahern Pass we detoured upward for half a mile onto the pass proper, a green saddle, then climbed another 1,300 feet up a steep field of rubble to Iceberg Notch. The craggy rock here reminded me of a distant city skyline. The notch is at peak level, a narrow gap in a wall of rock. It's an opening to the east, and also an opening for the nonstop west wind. We ate lunch in a sheltered corner just off a goat trail that edged the 1,600-foot drop to Iceberg Lake. While we ate, we looked at the scarred walls stained bright by lichens, stared down to the iceberg lumps on the lake, and with (Continued on page 193)

Swiftcurrent Mountain soars upward nearly 8,500 feet. A glacier nudges its northern flank, and a fire lookout's cabin sits on its wind-whipped summit, directly on the Continental Divide.

Fire lookout Brian Stricker scans the forest around Swiftcurrent Mountain for wisps of smoke. A 20-year-old student of social science at Evergreen State College in Olympia, Washington, Brian spent the summer of 1979 living here in the 14-by-14-foot hut. Cables secured to lichen-bright rocks stabilize the building during frequent high winds. Spotting smoke, Brian pinpoints its location with a firefinder (right) and radios the information to fire fighters in West Glacier. "My official hours are from 8 to 4:30," he says, "but since I'm here all the time, I'm 'on' all the time."

King of its realm, a mountain goat reigns over craggy heights. Flexible hooves,

a muscular torso, and short legs—ideal for balance—equip the goat for climbing.

At home on its range, a mule
deer grazes near Brown
Pass. A rich and varied
wildlife inhabits virtually
every elevation in Glacier.
Above, a mule deer buck, its
antlers sheathed in velvet,
pauses by the edge of a
lowland forest. A Columbian
ground squirrel stands by its
burrow in a valley.

binoculars tried to follow the movements of mitelike day hikers at the lake's edge far below.

Sandwiches and gorp were still spread on our laps when a clattering echoed above and behind us in the rocks. Before we could move, a mountain goat loped around the corner and onto the narrow ledge right at our feet. We were all equally surprised. She stopped and stared a second with black eyes, then leaped past us, sending a hail of rock chips off the cliff. She was followed by an equally startled kid and another adult. They hurried past, very white and very nimble on the loose, narrow ledge.

Two more long days of striding the trail in and out of one cirque after another took us over snowslides, across a vast, lushly watered meadow that was solid in some stretches with wild flowers, their saturated pastels a contrast to the patches of soiled snow. We stopped at cascades that were ideal for cooling and soaking our feet, and hiked past alarmist marmots, stolid toads, and bear scat. The second day ended at Kootenai Lakes, where we stopped to watch a cow moose and calf wading and feeding near the shore. Then it was only a short level hike through thick woods to Goat Haunt Ranger Station and the practical end of the trail.

We crossed a swinging bridge and stayed the night at a campsite on the Waterton River. On our final evening in camp, a six-point white-tailed buck calmly strolled out from the trees, stepped past our tent, and stopped for an investigatory sniff at the tuna-noodle casserole steaming on our stove.

To cap a trip of this magnitude, we felt, there should be something special at the end, and there is. The trail continues on around Waterton Lake and into Canada, but the option exists of taking a boat across the lake, a dark glacial cleft that extends through ranges of stark peaks for several miles across the border. So at Goat Haunt dock we paid our fares—back to civilization and the exchanging of money— and boarded the *International*, a white diesel-powered excursion boat. We shed our packs and sprawled on its windy deck to let the forest and the mountains glide past. It was a relief to be no longer measuring their passage with thousands of personal strides.

Ahead of us over the prow waited the Prince of Wales Hotel. It's a 1926 wooden château, and on its plain above the end of the lake it floats like a fairy-tale castle: surely an illustration and not a real place. But it was real, and the creaky interior held a welcome room with a bathtub, for a long soak, and a wicker chair in a high window, for a last long look down the dusky lake to the light at the ranger station, and beyond to the looming mountains of the Continental Divide.

Mike sheds his backpack for a seat with a view and relaxes on the deck of the International *during the final leg of his journey: a ninety-minute boat ride across Waterton Lake to Canada.*

FOLLOWING PAGES: *Warmly lit Prince of Wales Hotel beams a welcome as evening falls. Beyond Waterton Lake, jumbled peaks in the United States rise along the Continental Divide.*

Additional Reading

The reader may wish to consult the National Geographic Society Index for articles, and to refer to the following books. Carl Abbott, *Colorado: A History of the Centennial State*; Ruth W. Armstrong, *New Mexico: From Arrowhead to Atom*; Orville Bach, *Hiking the Yellowstone Backcountry*; Orrin and Lorraine Bonney, *Guide to the Wyoming Mountains and Wilderness Areas*; J. J. Brody, *Mimbres Painted Pottery*; T. Scott Bryan, *The Geysers of Yellowstone*; C. W. Buchholtz, *Man in Glacier*; Gloria Cline, *Exploring the Great Basin*; Mabel Crittenden and Dorothy Telfer, *Wildflowers of the West*; J. Gordon Edwards, *A Climber's Guide to Glacier National Park*; Laura Gilpin, *The Enduring Navajo*; Aubrey Haines, *The Yellowstone Story* (2 volumes); James Hamilton, *History of Montana: From Wilderness to Statehood*; Warren Hanna, *Montana's Many-Splendored Glacierland*; Bart Jackson, *White Water: Running the Wild Rivers of North America*; Joe Kelsey, *Climbing and Hiking in the Wind River Mountains*; Bank Langmore and Ron Tyler, *The Cowboy*; Taft Larson, *Wyoming: A History*; David Lavender, *David Lavender's Colorado*; Ward Alan Minge, *Acoma: Pueblo in the Sky*; Frank D. Reeve and Alice Ann Cleaveland, *New Mexico: Land of Many Cultures*; James E. and Barbara H. Sherman, *Ghost Towns and Mining Camps of New Mexico*; Clark Spence, *Montana: A History*; Spencer Wilson and Vernon J. Glover, *The Cumbres and Toltec Scenic Railroad*; James R. Wolf, *Guide to the Continental Divide Trail* (volumes 1 and 2); Ann H. Zwinger and Beatrice E. Willard, *Land Above the Trees: A Guide to American Alpine Tundra*.

Acknowledgments

The Special Publications Division is grateful to the individuals, organizations, and agencies named or quoted in the text and to those cited here for their generous assistance: Linda Bahm, Vernon C. Betts, Rodger Boyd, J. J. Brody, Dalton DuLac, Steve Dobrott, Fred Flint, Lew French, Michael G. Gardner, David Gaylord, David R. Grider, Robert L. Griffiths, Richard Guenzel, Richard Guth, Walter Harriman, Donald Heiser, A. H. Helgeson, Rodney Herrick, Jon F. Hollinger, Larry Irwin, Bill F. Isaacs, W. James Judge, Raymond Karr, Ralph Klawitter, JoAnn Korting, Tom Kovalicky, John H. Lancaster, Harry Leslie, Clyde M. Lockwood, Timothy Manns, Charles E. McConnell, Brainerd Mears, Al Mebane, Daniel Miller, Judd Moore, Robert Morey, Clif Palmer, Robert Perkins, Constance Poten, Sharon E. Prell, Barbara Roberts, Phil Roberts, Mac Roeber, Lester G. Scharnberg, John D. Schelberg, Biff Stransky, Robert H. Weber, and James R. Wolf; the Bureau of Land Management, the U. S. Forest Service, the National Park Service, and the Smithsonian Institution.

Index

Naturalist, teacher, guide, ranger, and author, Dr. J. Gordon Edwards draws on all his talents in Glacier National Park. A professor of entomology in California, Dr. Edwards also serves as a seasonal ranger in Glacier. He climbed most of the park's major peaks to compile A Climber's Guide to Glacier National Park. Here he leads hikers up Reynolds Mountain.

Library of Congress Cataloging in Publication Data
Robbins, Michael, 1938-
    High country trail.
    Bibliography: p.
    Includes index.
    1. Hiking—Rocky Mountains (U. S.) 2. Continental Divide Trail. 3. Natural history—Rocky Mountains. I. Chesley, Paul, 1946-   . II. National Geographic Society (U. S.). Special Publications Division. III. Title.
GV199.42.C84R6   796.5′22′0978   80-7826
ISBN 0-87044-361-5 (regular binding)   AACR2
ISBN 0-87044-366-6 (library binding)

Composition for *High Country Trail: Along the Continental Divide* by Composition Systems Inc., Arlington, Va., and National Geographic Photographic Services (index pages). Printed and bound by Holladay-Tyler Printing Corp., Rockville, Md. Color separations by The Beck Engraving Co., Philadelphia, Pa.; The Lanman Companies, Washington, D. C.; National Bickford Graphics, Inc., Providence, R.I.; Progressive Color Corp., Rockville, Md.

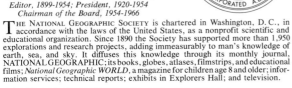